PLAIN ANNA

ANNA SCHWARTZ

First edition published by Blended Mix Publishing
Contact: www.blendedmixpublishing.com

Editor: Katie Chambers, Beacon Point Services

Internal photographs from the author's collection

Cover Design: Meg Delagrange-Belfon

PRINTED IN THE UNITED STATES OF AMERICA

Contents

To my eight children:
You are my greatest gift.

Forward

I have known Anna for most of her life, as she is my cousin by marriage. You'll discover, as you turn the pages of this book, that you'll come to know her as I have—she is a caring and compassionate soul. I can uniquely relate to her experiences because both of us were born and raised in the Amish culture.

Growing up as young girls, we were taught that we can do nothing without permission. We did as we were told, and we didn't question anything. It was natural for us to think we are "less than"—significantly less than men, less than the boys. We felt like we were valued less by our culture because we are females, and, therefore, our opinions, emotions, and ideas were insignificant. We were only allowed an eighth-grade education and were not given a chance to be ambitious. In our culture, having a career was not an option since a woman's place is considered at home in the role of a wife and mother.

As a result, we were raised to serve and please men. From an early age, it was ingrained deep within us to be submissive to our husbands, no matter what, even unto death. Even when our husbands abused us, we knew it would be pointless to object or try to leave.

Already traumatized by a brutal loss at a young age, Anna's story evolves from young romance turned into control, gross abuse, and confusion. She grew despondent, depressed, and desperately lost as her abuser steadily became more aggressive, controlling, and violent. After having her children, Anna felt stuck in her situation, helplessly witnessing terrible abuse extend to her children.

With the mindset of her upbringing, it's understandable how Anna could not defend herself in her marriage or adequately protect her children. When doubts entered her mind, she was taught to reject her misgivings about her culture or her husband. Through brainwashing and gaslighting, her suspicions were repeatedly replaced with twisted interpretations from the bible.

Eventually, Anna could no longer endure the control and abuse. As you read her true story, you will learn how she, at long last, escaped with her children from the pain and torment to a life of newfound freedom and victory. Anna finds the courage and strength to stand up and say, "NO MORE ABUSE. NO MORE FEAR!"

You'll find yourself cheering her on with great admiration for her courage and bravery. However, Anna didn't stop there. She sought healing and eventually became willing to relive the pain to write her story with the goal of helping others like her discover hope and strength. What a remarkable woman!

Bringing awareness to the effects of brainwashing and abuse is necessary in order to recognize when it's happening to us and when it's happening to someone else. That's why I highly encourage everyone to read this riveting, true story and pass it along to someone else. Each one of us can strike a match to hold a light in the shadows, together creating a bright flame that leads us to a better tomorrow.

Eirene Eicher

Best Selling Author of the *My Amish World* series

"Here is the world. Beautiful and terrible things will happen. Don't be afraid."
—Frederick Buechner

I.

HELLO FEAR

I met fear for the first time on the long, hard benches at *gma*, Sunday church. Mom had pinched my legs hard, so I sat rigidly still and listened to the *prediger*, the Amish preacher. His watery eyes nearly popped behind his thick bifocals as he preached about a terrifying *Gott in Himmel* from the *schrift*.

With as much zeal as his preaching, he reached into his pocket and pulled out a long white handkerchief to wipe the perspiration from his forehead. He was preaching so hard that a bit of foam started forming at the corners of his mouth, above his beard. He wiped that away too, momentarily, with the same white handkerchief before shoving it back into his *lots hussa.*

Gott in Himmel. Just the thought of that stern God glaring down from the heavens made me quiver, especially when I was alone.

Gott remembered every sin I had ever committed. The fear of *Gott* convinced me that I was irretrievably broken and unpardonable forever. I could not be cleansed. I could not be saved. I was doomed.

Perhaps, Mom had told me, the angels might let me into *Himmel* if I was good enough.

I met fear again on a dark night when I was seven years old. Mom was shaking me awake in my bed.

"Anna. Anna, *wach auff.*"

What was wrong? Why was Mom standing beside my bed?

"Anna, Anna, wake up. Uncle Joe's house is on fire." She made me get up.

I followed Mom downstairs and found the rest of my siblings huddled in front of the living room window. Standing on my tiptoes, I tried to see what they were looking at. In the distance, I could see a big ball of light. My uncle's house was on fire, Mom had said.

My sister Josephine started crying.

My cousin Betty's husband, Freeman, burst through the door, carrying his small baby into the house. "Somebody take the baby," he cried. "Quick! I have to go get Betty out of the house. I thought she was here, right behind me, but she's not!" Mom grabbed baby Andrew from Freeman's arms before he hurried back out.

Cousin Betty and Freeman lived at Uncle Joe's house, too. When they got married, they didn't have enough money saved up to buy a farm of their own so they lived with Betty's parents. This was not an uncommon situation for Amish families when I was growing up.

Since Amish youth give all of their wages to their mom and dad until they are twenty-one years old and many of them get married in their early twenties, not having enough money for a house of their own is common. So multiple generations of related family members often live together on the same homestead. Typically, the elderly parents live in a small house apart from the main house. It's usually called the *Dawdy Haus*.

On that fateful night, terror struck the hearts

of each person in our family as we watched Uncle Joe's house burn.

Freeman, filled with adrenaline, literally climbed up the side of their house to find my cousin Betty in the burning house. Once he got into the upstairs window, he searched for his young wife. He couldn't find her. The strength of the smoke and heat almost overcame him, so he had to go back out of the window. Uncle Joe helped him get down before they kept searching for the women who were still inside the burning house.

My single Aunt Leah, Uncle Joe's sister, also lived in the house. Her bedroom was in the back south corner of the house. Uncle Joe went around the house and knocked on her window to wake her up. Yelling against the glass, he tried to explain to her that the house was burning. He motioned for her to come over to the window so he could help her get out.

Confused, she got out of bed, but instead of coming to him, she went to her bedroom door, which opened into the living room. Perhaps she could hear Betty screaming. We'll never know.

The last thing any of us heard from Aunt Leah was her blood-curdling scream. She threw her hand over her mouth before running into the living room. The next day, we found her body lying next to the body of my cousin Betty.

It was a nightmare that I just wanted to wake up from. Filled with fear, we cried and hugged each other that night, trying to absorb the horrible truth that our minds simply could not comprehend. It was an unbelievable tragedy to lose two loved ones in one night.

I stood by the window with my siblings all night as we stared across the field and watched Uncle Joe's house burn down. How could this be happening? We continued watching as the fire trucks finally came. But it was too late. Nothing could be done to save Aunt Leah and Cousin Betty.

Aunt Leah was my favorite aunt, and Betty was my favorite cousin. They just could not be dead. No. I didn't want to believe any of it. My seven-year-old brain couldn't process what this meant.

Death. It was so final. So cold. From the moment I met Death, it made me feel helpless and alone.

I was in shock. I was afraid. Would *Gott in Himmel* send the fire to our house to punish us?

But it wasn't God who struck fire to Uncle

Joe's house. It was a resentful, troubled young man from our church, where Uncle Joe was the bishop. Since Uncle Joe wouldn't change the rules of the *Ordnung* to allow modern farming equipment, some men were very angry.

Angry enough to kill.

The police investigated and found evidence that someone had started the fire on the back porch of Uncle Joe's house. Additionally, they found tire tracks between the south of the farm and the road. Since we used horses and buggies, not cars, clearly, the young man had parked a borrowed car there. All of the evidence was pointing to him as the arsonist, the murderer of my beloved aunt and cousin.

Before the investigation could go any further, Uncle Joe refused to press charges. After all, we were Amish, and he was the bishop. As Amish, we were passivists. We wouldn't defend ourselves. We wouldn't go to war. We wouldn't take anyone to court. Because of this, he wouldn't press charges and no one would cooperate with the murder investigation.

And so, the case was dropped.

Ten days after Uncle Joe's house burned to the ground, my only remaining grandma passed away. Still in shock from losing Aunt Leah and Cousin Betty, I watched everyone around me crumble under the fresh news of yet another death. Grief filled my young soul like thick, suffocating back tar. An eternal sadness seemed to sink deep into the depths of my soul, clouding my world with a fog that wouldn't go away.

By Amish tradition, mourning a death takes a long time. The immediate family of the person who died must wear black for six months. Since my family had lost three loved ones, we were expected to wear black for at least a year and a half, or longer.

Black just seemed like such a sad color. I hated wearing it every single day.

Seeing my mom wearing black each day filled me with fear too. That dark, suffocating tar of grief had permeated everyone and everything around me. I was so afraid of Death. Death felt so close, like it might reach its claws around the bed one night and snatch me in my sleep. Or it would take Mom. Or Dad.

Oh.

I couldn't bear the thought of losing my parents. I would rather have Death take me than them. When thunderstorms came at night, I was afraid. I'd always been afraid of storms because Dad was afraid of them, but now sheer terror filled my thoughts when I saw the lightning strike the air and a loud crack of thunder shook our house. Maybe lightning would strike our house and light it on fire. Nothing felt safe anymore.

With all that fear and darkness, I had a hard time being happy. Sadness seemed to follow me everywhere I went. In the fall, I started my second year of school and trudged there in my black dress, knowing that everyone felt sad when they looked at me. Sometimes the kids were mean and laughed at me.

Fear. Sadness. That was my life.

Our Amish church was in a lot of turmoil. Grievances had stacked up against Uncle Joe: he was too conservative for everyone's liking. The men in the church were still angry. They still wanted him to change the rules of the *Ordnung*. Other Amish churches had begun to allow a few more modern conveniences, such as more modern farming equipment that would help them farm more land to provide a better living for their families.

Since Uncle Joe was our bishop, it was up to him to help change the age-old rules. But he refused to do that. He wouldn't even consider changing the rules that protected our way of life. He stood on the shoulders of our Anabaptist ancestors who burned at the stake for what they believed in. It's doubtful that they would have chosen to burn over a decision between tractors or a horse-drawn plow, but for Uncle Joe, it was quite literally a decision worth dying for. Instead of changing his beliefs, he decided to move his family to a new, strict Old Order Amish community in New York.

When Uncle Joe and his family moved away, it felt like another death. We had bonded so closely through the grief and kinship that we shared. After their house burned down, they moved in with my family for a while. It was a bright spot in my life to play with my cousin John, who was just a little older than me. Sometimes my sister and I played dress-up with baby Andrew. All of us girls gathered around him to become stand-in mamas for him after cousin

Betty died. After all, we were family, and we took care of our own.

None of us felt welcome at *gma*, church, anymore. But my parents were not ready to move as far away as Uncle Joe did. So they decided that we would move to another, smaller community about twenty miles north.

It was a huge adjustment. Everyone was a stranger there, and I had to go to a new school. It was hard. We still had to wear our black mourning clothes to every church service and all social gatherings, but my siblings and I were allowed to wear a couple other dark colors to school, like dark blue and dark green.

When the Christmas program was being planned that fall, I begged Mom for a new dress to wear for the program. She said that we were still in mourning, so we still needed to wear black to all church services and social Amish gatherings. I was so sad. Grief still permeated everything, burdening everyone, even in this new world that we had moved to.

On the day of the Christmas program, my mom and older sisters were whispering a lot. When I came into a room, they would quit talking. My two oldest sisters, Esther and Betty, looked knowingly at me before hurrying outside to finish up their chores. I could not figure out what was going on, and I was so curious. I tried pestering my sisters to find out what they knew, but no one would tell me anything.

When it was time to dress for the program, my mom took me into the living room and handed me a new dress. I could not believe it! Finally, I had another color to wear! My new dress was a creamy brown color. Now, you might think that a brown dress might not seem like such a difference, but it was for me. I was finally allowed to go to a social gathering wearing a color other than black.

Mom had cut my new dress from a silky knit fabric that felt like butter in my hands. It was stitched together with tiny, perfect stitches. Around the waist, it had neatly laid, ironed pleats.

Oh, how pretty I felt that night in my new brown dress. My hair was freshly washed, parted in the center and braided back into a slick bun underneath a crisp white Amish covering. I wasn't allowed to feel beautiful, because that would be prideful and pride is a grave sin, but it felt nice to feel just a little bit pretty.

I still remembered the day I'd asked Mom why

we couldn't wear more colors, why we had to dress so plain. She quoted Psalm 27:11 to me: "Teach me thy way, O Lord, and lead me in a plain path." Explaining that, according to Amish tradition, our literal plain ways were an act of obedience to scripture. I accepted that explanation, especially because I wanted to please *Gott in Himmel.*

On top of wearing black, I had the awful experience of being laughed at. Especially by one of my cousins, Esther. I was fat and Esther was skinny. She was always asking me how much I weighed. At school, the kids laughed at me too. I was so ashamed of how I looked, and I wanted to hide. The embarrassment of it all weighed me down more than my body did.

———————

We only lived in that Amish community for about a year. More and more people were moving to New York, where my Uncle Joe and his family now lived, including some of my parents' closest friends.

When my parents decided to move there too, I was quite excited by the thought of having a new adventure and a new life.

A new life far away from black dresses and sadness. Far away from anything that could make me feel afraid.

2.

SAMUEL

Spring 1977

My family moved to a 160-acre farm in the hills of upstate New York. I thought the hills were the most beautiful sight I had ever seen. In Indiana, where we lived before, everything was endlessly flat as far as the eye could see. Not here. Nothing in New York was as plain as Indiana. In our new house, we had a big picture window in our living room where we could see the smoky blue Adirondack Mountains in the distance.

While this community was much smaller than the ones I had lived in before, it was better, as life finally seemed to have less sadness, and I soon made a best friend. I loved going to school and sharing secrets with her.

Being part of such a small community, we heard all the gossip about everyone else. One person that was mentioned in a lot of the gossip was a young man by the name of Samuel Troyer. The Troyer family had moved to New York from Pennsylvania. I heard stories about how his dad wasn't nice to him, and it seemed he was very troubled.

I felt sorry for Samuel Troyer. Because I had been bullied when we lived in Indiana, I knew how it felt to be looked down on and made fun of. So I would smile at him and try to say hi to him sometimes, even though I was shy.

While I was ten years old and he was twenty, I wasn't too young to notice his handsome features when his moody eyes met mine. They brightened just for a brief moment. He had strong arms and warm olive-colored skin. His thick black hair was wavy, coiling up and away from his ears even after it was combed and smoothed down. The traditional bowl cut for an Amish man's hair is designed to keep their hair below their ears, a subtle keeping to modesty. Samuel's hair rebelled against that tradition.

As I grew into my teen years, I began stretching out. My awkward body started taking shape as it became more womanly. Losing weight made me feel a little better about myself, and I could tell that others looked at me differently, too.

In September, I turned sixteen, which meant I could begin attending youth gatherings. This is the season to discover our independence. It's called *Rumspringa*. In our Old Order Amish community, this meant that a young person was free to explore a few things in the outside world before becoming a member of the Amish church. Each weekend, the youth would gather at a home or in a barn to sing and socialize. In different communities, these gatherings have different names. We called the weekly social gathering a *singing*, and I couldn't wait to go. I had older siblings who were already in *Rumspringa*, and a few that had already gotten married.

By the time I was old enough to be part of *Rumspringa*, my older brother had gotten married and settled down with his wife. Since my younger sisters and I no longer had a brother and we didn't have any Amish neighbors nearby that we could ride with, we took ourselves with Dad's horse and buggy. It was embarrassing to go out to the barn after a *singing* and get our horse to hitch him to the buggy because we were the only girls with all of those boys. Hitching up a horse was not a woman's job, but we had no other choice.

My first taste of independence bolstered my confidence. The world began to feel like something I might be able to take on and conquer. I really enjoyed going to the weekly singing, where all of us would sit and sing German hymns together. On warm afternoons, my best friend and I loved playing volleyball and softball.

We saved a little of the money we got from cleaning the homes of Englishers to buy a disposable camera, and we gave the rest of our earnings to Dad and Mom. In the Amish culture, it is an unspoken understanding that youth are to give all of their earnings to their parents until they reach the age of twenty-one, or until they get married. Buying the camera was our little secret, as cameras were forbidden.

The *Ordnung* quoted one of the ten commandments as proof that taking or having photos is a sin: "Thou shalt not make unto thee any graven image." It was the third commandment given to Moses on a stone tablet in the Old Testament. This scripture was incorrectly translated from the original context of forbidding the worship of inanimate idols and heretofore applied to the act of capturing an image of oneself on film.

Not seeing the harm in taking a photo, we waited until we were away from home to pull out the forbidden camera and take pictures of each other. It was a surreal feeling to hold a developed stack of prints in my hands. There I was, in a photo. My face was printed on a glossy piece of paper. Once the fun wore off, guilt set in. I thought I was going to hell for having a graven image in my possession.

Even though we did our best to keep it hidden, Mom found the camera and made us break it up with a hammer. I wondered if God's wrath felt like a hammer as the plastic pieces splintered into small pieces under the blunt force of the hammer.

———

In December, it was our turn to have *gma*, the bi-weekly Amish church service, at our house. We spent weeks preparing for it. Everything was cleaned and scrubbed, from the upstairs bedrooms to the basement. The windows were washed inside and out, even though the temperatures were freezing. No effort was spared in making our home shine.

On the day of *gma*, we got up early in the morning to set up benches and tables throughout the house. Men would be kept segregated from the women throughout the day, so in each room, the benches were placed in two groupings on opposite sides from each other. My sisters and I had spent our Saturday baking dozens of loaves of bread for Sunday. We also mixed up a generous amount of creamy peanut butter with marshmallow cream. We called that delicious mixture Amish peanut butter.

The traditional Amish church lunch is bread, Amish peanut butter, jam, pickles, pickled red beets, coffee, and tea.

In the evening, the young folks and a few families were invited to come back to our house for supper. Not dinner. Supper. The Amish called the evening meal supper, always. I can't tell you why. That's just what we called it. The Englishers called supper, dinner. We were not like the *Englisha*. We were a peculiar people, a set apart people.

The traditional, main Amish meal for us was

mashed potatoes, gravy, burned butter noodles, vegetables, bread and butter, and meatloaf. For dessert, we served mixed fruit in Jello, cake, and pies.

That night after supper, the young people sat around the table and sang from a German hymnal for an hour or two. Because a Sunday isn't a true Sunday without popcorn, my older sisters popped big bowls of popcorn for everyone to enjoy. Then my younger sisters and I entertained everyone by yodeling in harmony to Swiss songs we had learned from Dad.

When the last colors of the setting sun had faded into dusk, the men began to go out and hitch up the horses to the buggies. Taking turns, they pulled up to the house to pick up the girls. If someone was dating, he would take the girl to her house, then stay there for a date, usually sitting at the kitchen table.

As everyone was getting ready to leave, Samuel came over and asked if he could stay, to see me. I was surprised but flattered. I was only sixteen and he was twenty-six. But with warm cheeks, I said yes.

———————

Because my parents didn't want me dating at

such a young age, they tried to get my sisters and other family members to talk to me. They all felt that I should not get too serious with someone, that I should simply enjoy being young. Go out with the youth. Have fun with my best friend. Explore my options.

Being so young and inexperienced, I didn't understand why they were so concerned. I thought Samuel was being so nice to me. What could be the harm in dating him?

In the beginning, it was a fairytale. Each week Samuel bought me a gift when he came to see me. Chocolates. Fancy perfume in a crystal bottle from the department store. Shiny, black leather gloves. A keychain with my name on it. Luxurious house shoes. And more chocolates. He never came without bringing me something. I drowned in the intensity of his eyes and his expressive declarations of love.

I was living in an intoxicating dream, and I only wanted more.

My intoxication was fueled by Patricia Williams, the fanciest lady that my sisters and I ever cleaned house for, who had a home that felt like a castle. *Eyiyie*. And one day she came to our house for supper.

We spent two days preparing the house for our special visitor. Patricia Williams is from South Africa, and we had never had a visitor from another country in our home before.

Early in the morning on the day of, we put large vats of water on the stove to heat before heading outside to butcher some chickens for supper. Mom had her own efficient system for butchering chickens. Once their heads were off, we poured boiling water into five-gallon buckets and dipped the chickens in the buckets. The boiling water made it easier to pull their feathers out. Together, my sisters and I made quick work of readying the meat.

Homemade white bread, mashed potatoes, gravy, and buttered green beans were also on the menu. For dessert, we would serve warm peach pie and homemade ice cream. Oh, it was going to be a treat of a meal.

Since I wanted Patricia to meet Samuel, I invited him over, too. I picked out my creamiest pastel dress to wear that evening—light blue—with a freshly ironed, snowy white cape and apron. I pinned the *shatz banlah*, a wide fabric belt that matched my dress, snuggly around my waist. My cheeks burned when I admired my trim figure in the mirror before I hurried down the stairs.

Patricia Williams had a royal air about her; maybe it was the way her accent sounded British to me. She seemed just as curious about our life as I was about hers. I tried not to stare as I noticed everything about her outfit. I was so plain compared to her.

She wore large, shiny pearls set about with tiny sparkling diamonds in her ears. Her velvety green dress had a darted bodice with a fitted waist that dropped to a flared midi skirt. On her feet, she wore a pair of white heels. I couldn't help but think about how quickly those shoes would turn from white to brown if Patricia had to get in and out of a buggy on a rainy day.

Then a knock at the door interrupted my thoughts. Samuel. I felt my heart racing as he came into the house. He removed his hat as soon as he saw Patricia. Smiling widely, he introduced himself to her as he shook her hand with a visibly comfortable demeanor.

Wow, I never knew Samuel had such nice manners. Throughout the evening, he carried on conversations with Patricia with ease. He knew just how to act around the *Englisha*. I was impressed.

Patricia was impressed with Samuel too. The next time my sisters and I went to her house to clean it, she couldn't stop talking about him.

"What a lovely young man, such nice manners," she said. "Such a bright mind he has, the way he thinks is so innovative. And he's very handsome. Anna, you've got a good one; he's a keeper!"

My cheeks blushed as I nodded.

———————

Samuel's moody demeanor returned after his parents had a fight. His parents seemed to fight a lot, unlike mine. One night we sat at the kitchen table, and he put his head down on his folded arms in a dejected slump. He seemed deeply troubled and depressed. He admitted to me that he felt like ending his life. This shocked me. Determined to lift his spirits, I listened and rubbed his back to comfort him.

My compassion for Samuel ran deep. For six years I had carried compassion in my heart for him, since the first time I saw him when I was only ten years old. I wanted to comfort him. I wanted to be a safe person for him to talk to, no matter what.

Soon Samuel wanted the two of us to spend all of our free time together, and I knew it was because he loved me so much. Eventually, though, he no longer wanted us to hang out with my best friend. I was sad about that. I loved my best friend so much, but when I tried to talk to Samuel about it, he got moody and angry.

The next time we were together, he gave me a lavish gift. Samuel had asked his mom how much fabric was needed to make a dress with a matching cape and apron. Then he chose multiple colors of special fabric from Ohio and had it shipped to New York.

It was enough fabric to make not just one but six new dresses: dark green, light green, dark blue, light blue, a deep turquoise, and rich chocolate brown. His peace offering was a whole new wardrobe!

Not wanting to seem ungrateful, I accepted his gift and decided to just let go of my desire to spend time with my best friend.

I completely missed the bouquets of red flags that Samuel kept handing to me. My parents could see the red flags, however, and they were devising a plan.

3.

A School Teacher

Late summer 1984

Dad and Mom had arranged for me to go teach school for my cousins in Michigan, hoping to get me away from Samuel. They asked him not to visit during the school year, but we would still be allowed to write to each other.

My cousin's community had a one-room schoolhouse for all eight grades. In Amish communities, an eighth-grade education is considered enough of "book learning." No one finished high school or went to college. That would have been worldly. After one turns thirteen years old, they continue their education by working in the family trade until they reach adulthood.

Boys learned to do whatever their dad did. Farming. Raising produce to take to the markets. Construction work.

Girls learned whatever their mom did. Quilting. Sewing. Making baked goods to sell. Butchering chickens. Cleaning house for the *Englisha*.

Though I was only sixteen when the school year started, just slightly older than the eighth-grade boys, I would turn seventeen in September. And so it was decided that I was old enough to become a teacher. Most of the students were my cousins, and I could only imagine what a fun adventure this was going to be.

The day before the *Engilsha* driver came to pick me up to drive me to Michigan, I went over everything I had packed one more time. I'd never been away from home for such a long time before, and I wanted to make sure I wasn't forgetting anything that I should take with me. A few other people would be joining me on the trip, to split the cost of hiring a driver. Once we got to Michigan, he would pick up Amish folks that wanted to travel back with him to New York.

Early in the morning, the driver came. Dad

and Mom were up to see me off. Dad slipped some spending money into my hand and patted my shoulder.

"Write to us," Mom said.

I promised that I would.

And then, with both excitement and a knot in my stomach, I climbed into the van and watched my home disappear around the bend in the rolling hills.

———————

When I caught a glimpse of where I would teach school, I fell in love. It was a cute little white schoolhouse under a huge maple tree down a gravel road. It was close enough to my cousin's house for me to walk there. Behind the schoolhouse was a flat green area where we'd play ball for recess. Close to the schoolhouse, they had a small swing set for the younger children to swing on. Around the corner were the outhouses for everyone to go to the bathroom.

Inside the schoolhouse, there was a small front room with hooks and benches where the students could hang their coats and store their lunchboxes for the day. A shiny red hand water pump stood in the back right corner of the schoolroom, so we could get water to drink. Next to the water pump was a wall full of hooks to hang colorful plastic cups by their little round handles.

Near the center of the room sat the most adorable little potbellied stove. Every school morning, I went in early to start a fire, and I kept it going throughout the day to keep us all warm.

I imagined that I was Laura Ingalls, a character from my favorite series of books, *Little House on the Prairie*, set in the late 1800s. Laura's family joined the early settlers that moved out west, where she taught school in a one-room schoolhouse. Laura's way of life was so similar to my own.

I had a lot of fun that fall and winter. Each week I prepared lessons and kept the schoolhouse organized and tidy for my students. I loved teaching. There was something so invigorating about it all. Recess was a lively time for all of us. Every day I went outside to play softball and volleyball with my students. They fought over whose team I'd play ball on, so I took turns playing on different teams to be fair.

Inside the classroom, my students also fought for my attention, and I let each one think that they were my favorite. Since it was such a small school, I could spend one-on-one time with each of them. They often brought me cookies or apples or some tasty homemade treats. Sometimes the treats were homemade cards, even the older boys made a few for me. I was their favorite teacher. They said so. And I knew it was true.

During the winter, the students brought soup in little steel containers for their lunches, paired with sandwiches wrapped in tinfoil. They would keep their eyes on the clock, and about a half-hour before lunchtime, they would ask if they could go to their lunchboxes and get their food to put on the stovetop. Pretty soon, the whole room would smell mouthwatering, and we would all feel very hungry for lunch.

After lunch recess, I would read a chapter from a book in the liveliest tone I could imagine for each character in the story. Most days, I read two chapters because the children kept begging for me to read more. I gave in easily because we all wanted to find out what would happen next.

Samuel wrote to me every week, and I wrote back to him. I made sure my letters didn't reflect all the fun I was having because I didn't want him to feel jealous. Instead, I wrote about how much I missed him.

Truthfully, I didn't know it would feel so good to be on my own. My taste for independence was growing, and it was glorious.

Soon my cousins begged me to go with them to their youth gatherings. But Samuel had asked me not to go. So even though he was hundreds of miles away, I respected his wishes and stayed at home on Sunday evenings. It was the perfect time for me to read books or go on walks.

Samuel did not honor my parents' wishes and came to see me at Christmas. He begged me to come home with him so we could get married. Again, I was shocked. While it is true the Amish got married young, I was only seventeen. Trembling, because I didn't want to make him angry, I explained to him that I really wanted to finish teaching till the end of the year, so he finally went home without me.

I was so worried about Samuel. I felt so conflicted. As much as I loved teaching school and being on my own, I worried he wouldn't be okay. It weighed heavily on me, so I wrote home often. Whenever I got a new gift in the mail, I was comforted and hoped that everything would turn out alright.

But then his letters to me were troubled and suicidal. Distraught that he might hurt himself, I lost a lot of weight. I was stressed out, thinking that he might really kill himself. I was no longer getting my period because I was underweight, so my cousins were also worried about my health.

Samuel came again in March. This time I didn't enjoy his visit at all. From the moment he arrived, he began putting pressure on me to go home with him so we could get married. I was too worn out to resist and stand up to him. So, I finally said yes.

And so this dance with fear had become the rhythm of our courtship. When I wasn't sure about something, Samuel would win me over with gifts. When he spoke of having thoughts of committing suicide, I was so scared I did anything to try to make him happy again. But it was never enough for long.

Our relationship felt exhausting from the constant highs and lows. It was confusing. It was a web that I couldn't seem to get out of.

When we got home, I could tell that my parents weren't happy with my decision. I was torn in two. I felt so guilty and ashamed to leave my cousins without a teacher. But my fear of what Samuel might do if I didn't come home with him was greater. My parents didn't say much to me. Instead, they sent my sister to Michigan to finish teaching for the rest of the school year.

It didn't take long for Samuel to ask my parents if we could get married. I was only seventeen, so, of course, they said no. They asked us to wait till I was eighteen.

Oh, I had never seen Samuel get so angry. "Listen, Anna, if they, if your dad tries to split us up"—he spit into the ground—"I'll beat him up."

I was crying and terrified. "Please, Sam, please don't." But there was nothing I could do to calm him down.

There was a dark, wild look in his eyes when he left that night. I thought back to the night when he first asked me for a date. I replayed that Sunday evening over and over in my mind, wistfully remembering my naivety and fleeting, precious freedom. I wished I had just said no. But now, I was afraid that if I broke up with him, he would kill himself or hurt my dad, and it would be my fault.

Feeling lost, I went into the house. I didn't tell my sisters how I felt. Instead, I cried myself to sleep. I was ashamed and too afraid to admit my true feelings to anyone. I didn't want to betray his confidence in me. Even though I was now afraid of him, I felt a deep need to protect him at all costs.

———————

Summer came again, and with it, brighter times.

I was *following church*, as we say, which means that I was studying the eighteen Articles of Faith of the Amish church so that I could officially become a member. A group of us, all close to the same age, studied together each week. During the week, we memorized large sections by heart so we could recite them on Sunday. We would meet with the Amish preachers in an upstairs room every Sunday morning before going downstairs for the service.

A few weeks before our baptism service, Mom let me drink a beer for the first time. It was a part of *Rumspringa* that I had not experienced before. I didn't really care for the taste of it, so I drank the whole bottle of Blue Ribbon beer really fast to get it over with.

Almost instantly I felt sick, and my family started laughing at me. Soon I was laughing, and I didn't even know why. I got up because I wanted to go outside, but I just couldn't get to the door, which made all of us laugh some more.

Once outside, I lay down on the grass and looked up at the sky. The ground felt like it was tipping, so I spread out my arms to steady myself. I closed my eyes as my head pounded. The wet dew from the grass soaked the back of my dress as I inhaled the evening air.

I felt deliciously alive.

My sisters had asked me if I wanted to invite Samuel over, but I didn't want him to be there that night. I felt like I couldn't be myself around him. Whenever I was having a good time with others, he became moody and jealous. And I was afraid he would punish me for doing something worldly like drinking beer. He was already twenty-seven and a baptized member of the church, so his days of sowing any wild oats were long gone.

I kept hoping that if I married Samuel, he would know how much I loved him, and he would finally quit threatening to kill himself. We could start a new life together and be happy. I had hope that we would be happy and he would respect me because he had talked a lot about how his dad treated his mom. He got emotional about this, because it wasn't right, and he would tell me that he would never mistreat me like his dad did his mom.

4.

A Wife

September 1985

We got married four days after my eighteenth birthday.

When an Amish couple plan to get married, it is kept a secret. Only our parents and siblings could know that we were going to get married. I also told my best friend and wrote letters to our relatives in Indiana and Michigan, inviting them to come to the wedding. But other than that, there would be no formal wedding invitations.

Two weeks before our wedding, Samuel and I went to see the bishop. We told him we wanted to get married. The bishop pursed his lips before he began asking us some questions.

"Yes." Samuel nodded. "We've already talked to our parents. They gave us their blessing to get married."

"Are there any problems, errr, sins you need to confess?" the bishop asked.

"No."

I squirmed in my seat. It didn't feel like we were being honest, but it wasn't my place to speak up, so I remained silent.

The bishop, satisfied with the answers Samuel gave him, nodded his approval. He would announce our upcoming marriage, the date, and place at the next gma. Everyone in the community was automatically invited. Once the wedding was announced, everyone put everything else aside. There was a wedding to plan!

In our culture, it was an honor to be asked to help with any part of a wedding. That's why all of the youth from Rumspringa looked forward to serving the tables during the meal at our wedding and finding out who they might be paired up with. It was almost like an Amish version of prom. Often new couples emerged from a wedding, after a day of serving together and having fun!

Our closest neighbors in the community offered to host our wedding in their home. It was cus-
tomary for the female relatives of the bride to prepare
the food. Even though it was a lot of work, my mom,
my sisters, and Aunt Susie, Uncle Joe's wife, were excited to prepare all the food for the wedding day. It
would be an extra special meal, with grilled steak and
layered chocolate pudding for everyone who sat at the
bridal table with the bride and groom.

———————

A week before the wedding, I finished sewing
the cape and apron for my wedding dress and tried it
on. I'd chosen a deep, navy blue fabric for my dress.
Satisfied with the way it fit my body, I ironed it carefully and hung it up for the wedding day.

My older sister, who was already married, had
come by the house that morning. She admired the
fabric of my dress, waiting until Mom left the room
to lean over and ask me how I was feeling about what
would happen in the bedroom after the wedding.

I blushed and shrugged my shoulders. We
never talked about sex in my family, so I was embar-

rassed that my sister was mentioning it.

"When it's time, just relax." She looked at me knowingly. "If you relax, it feels better."

On the morning of the wedding, I remembered my sister's words as I looked in the mirror. I woke up with a knot in my stomach and wondered if it was normal to feel so nervous. I fought the feeling that wanted to suffocate me, the reality that life as I'd known it was changing again. I was going to be a married woman. Staring at my reflection, I searched my own face for a bit of reassurance that everything was going to be wonderful in my new life but found fear in my eyes instead. I glanced out the window and thought about running away.

Just relax, my sister's words echoed in my head.

My sisters were already at the house where our wedding would be held, setting up all the tables. Each place setting was decorated with napkins embossed with our names, Samuel and Anna, and our wedding date. Above our names, a pair of tiny bluebells was centered in a dainty wreath of flowers. I'd never seen prettier napkins. Wedding napkins, in Amish tradition, doubled as a wedding favor. The *corner table,* or the bridal table, would be set with new china and glassware that would then be given to us for our new home. There would be a big layered wedding cake with bowls of fresh fruit on each side, along with two candles set in small, crystal candleholders.

With all this preparation, I couldn't run away. It wouldn't be right. I exhaled and cinched the crisp white apron band around my waist.

Relax, I told myself.

During the two-hour wedding *gma,* my nerves were replaced with hunger pangs. We could all smell the mouthwatering aroma of food that was waiting to be served at the reception.

I forced myself to focus and listen to the bishop's droning voice as he recounted a story from one of the lost books of the Bible where a couple got married, had sex the first night, and later that night, the bridegroom died. It was Amish tradition to include this tale at a wedding as an instruction to the young couple to wait three nights after the wedding to consummate their marriage.

Squirming a little in my seat and straightening my back, I snuck a glance at Samuel. He met my eyes and gave me a nervous smile. That made me feel better. Perhaps marriage wouldn't be so bad after all, if I didn't starve before we got to the meal. I was so hungry I felt faint.

A special meal had been prepared for the corner table. Steak for lunch and a special dessert from our *Englisha* neighbor, called Robert Redford Dessert. It had a graham cracker crust topped with cool whip, cream cheese, and chocolate pudding. *Delicious.* I'd never tasted anything so wonderful.

Around us, the room filled with the buzz of conversation as everyone laughed and talked between bites of food. For the first time that day, I felt myself relaxing. My best friend sat near me at the corner table, and we snuck in small conversations with each other.

We spent the afternoon visiting with our guests. The children ran outside to play until it was time to leave with their parents. The young people from *Rumspringa* stayed for an evening meal of pizza. Finally, we cut our cake and shared it. Someone got out a hymn book, and we sang our favorite German songs late into the night.

There was no honeymoon. The day after the wedding, we helped our family clean up everything from the day before and put the house back in order.

———————

After our wedding, we moved in with Samuel's parents. We lived in one part of the house, and they lived in the other. I wasn't sure how I would like being so close to his parents, but I was excited to set up house with my new husband.

About a week after we moved into our part of the house, we hired an *Englisha* driver to take us grocery shopping. I was thrilled at the thought of filling our cupboards with my own spices as I donned my bonnet and shawl for the trip to town.

I had made a list of everything I needed to start making meals for my husband. Our driver dropped us off at the grocery store, and we started going up and down the aisles. Oh my, I had so many choices! I began happily selecting the spices, my mouth already starting to water as I thought about making some of the new recipes from one of the cookbooks we had gotten for a wedding present.

Preoccupied with this exciting adventure, I didn't notice that Samuel had begun lagging behind me. When I looked back to show him something, he was no longer with me or the cart. That's when I saw him lying down on the floor in the middle of the store aisle.

I blinked. Was I imagining this? But no, I wasn't. Samuel was lying on the floor, curling his legs up in a fetal position.

And that's not all. He was crying.

What on earth is happening, I wondered. I went over to him, concerned that he was sick. That's the only explanation my mind gave me for what was going on with my new husband.

"Sam," I whispered. "*Vas is letz?* What's wrong? Are you okay?"

He didn't answer me, but I heard a groan.

"*Vas is letz?*" I repeated.

He finally told me that I was spending too much money on groceries.

I was absolutely horrified and ashamed. People were staring at us. We already stood out as Amish, and now we were being stared at by the *Englisha* as my new husband laid on the floor in the middle of the grocery store aisle and cried because I was spending too much money on groceries.

After that, I was always afraid to spend money.

Long gone were the days when Samuel doted on me with generous gifts. Even just buying the bare necessities triggered an outburst of anger and loud scolding from my husband.

———————

Before we got married, Dad and Mom asked that we wait at least one year before trying to get pregnant. My parents were concerned about me getting pregnant too young because I have scoliosis. While I had been going to regular chiropractic treatments, and my body was responding well to the treatments, they advised me to wait until I was a little older and had my back in a straighter position before going through pregnancy.

Samuel agreed and promised my parents that we would wait. Mom took me to a doctor, and I got started on the pill.

About a week before the wedding, Samuel told me to quit taking the pill. I was confused. He seemed restless and worried. Concerned, I asked him why he changed his mind. It would be dangerous for me to get pregnant too soon.

By quoting some Bible verses, Samuel claimed that it would be a sin to prevent pregnancy. He showed me a story from Genesis 38. A man named Onan was not willing to impregnate his brother's widow in order to continue on the bloodline, so he masturbated and spilled his sperm into the ground. In the biblical tale, *Gott in Himmel* took Onan's life. Samuel interpreted that story in the literal sense that *Gott in Himmel* would be angry if we used birth control to prevent a pregnancy.

Fearing Samuel's wrath and *Gott in Himmel*, I quit taking the pill. It shouldn't have been a surprise when I got pregnant soon after we got married. Similar to the way a young girl feels like a stranger in her changing body at puberty, I felt lost in mine. I was barely a woman, and here I was growing a new little life inside of me.

Since we got married, I no longer cleaned houses for the *Englisha* with my sisters. Not having this job made me feel lonely. I missed my family, especially my sisters. Even though I felt miserable from having morning sickness, I longed to work with them again. When we went to have Sunday supper with my family after *gma*, my parents could see how I felt, so they convinced Samuel to let me continue cleaning houses with my sisters.

Cleaning houses with my sisters distracted me from how I was feeling. We were really close, so we had fun spending time together. We enjoyed learning about the life of the *Englisha* through organizing their magazines, listening to their music on the radio, and watching small snippets of movies or shows on their TVs. We even bought a new camera when we had the chance and took photos of each other, like old times.

In December, my parents invited us to go with them to visit one of my older sisters and her family in Michigan. The last time I'd seen them was when I taught school for our cousins. Oh, I so wanted to go on this trip. Samuel didn't want to go, but he reluctantly agreed to let me go with my parents and two of my sisters.

A few days after we got to Michigan, I got a call at my sister's neighbor's house from Samuel. The Amish don't have phones in their houses. Back then, we went to our *Englisha* neighbors if we needed to make a call. Today that has changed, and most Amish families have a *phone shack* outside where they are allowed to have a phone.

I ran across the road to my sister's neighbor's house and called Samuel, who was at our neighbor's house back in New York waiting for me to call. I had no idea what was going on at home. From the tone of his voice, I knew that something was up.

"Anna, I called a Mennonite minister in Kentucky. His name is JR Troyer."

"Okay," I responded, unsure of where this conversation was going. Why was Samuel talking to a Mennonite minister? We didn't have anything to do with the Mennonites, even though our beliefs were similar. When people left the Amish and joined the Mennonites, they were excommunicated and shunned.

Samuel coughed and then kept talking, "They left the Amish a few years ago. JR and his wife."

I remained silent, a knot growing in my stomach. I wasn't prepared for what Samuel would say next.

"JR is on his way up here to help us move to Kentucky. I bought a truck, and my mom is helping me pack up our stuff. So when you get home, we will be moving to Kentucky."

Reeling, I steadied myself against the counter and pressed the phone to my ear. Had I heard Samuel correctly? We were leaving the Amish? Moving to Kentucky?

How could I even tell my parents this news? How would they ever accept it? If you were born Amish, you stayed Amish. That was how I was raised. That was how I believed. That was how I wanted to raise our family. I felt sick, sicker than when I had morning sickness. I crossed the road back to my sister's house, slowly this time.

My sisters knew something was wrong by the look on my face. They followed me upstairs where we would be alone so we could talk. I told them what Samuel had done and what was happening. They were just as shocked as I was. How could this be happening? We all hugged each other and cried.

Life as I had always known it was coming to an end, and I could do nothing to stop the change from happening. During the rest of our trip, I treasured every moment that I spent with my family. I knew that if Samuel and I really did leave the Amish, we would be excommunicated and my family would not be allowed to have us in their home anymore.

As the wheels of the *Englisha* driver's van turned to take us back to New York, I remembered my last trip from Michigan to New York. The one where Samuel convinced me to quit teaching school and marry him. A lump rose in my throat and threatened to choke me as my tears spilled silently into my lap. Samuel and I had never even discussed leaving the Amish. How could he just decide our future without first discussing it with me?

Spouses should consult each other. While my parents were far from perfect and didn't always agree on things, they did discuss with each other before making big decisions. By Amish tradition, the man is the head of the family and so makes the final decision. But my parents taught me by their example to discuss major decisions together. In that way, Dad respected Mom's ideas.

I felt heartbroken. I was not prepared to take this step with Samuel. I was not ready to make such a huge decision, nor to have such a decision made for me without my knowledge or consent. This unchangeable circumstance felt unforgivable.

Watching the world slip by in a blur outside my window, I could also see my own world disappearing.

5.

A MOTHER

June 12, 1986

The day started peacefully that morning in up-state New York. Soft, golden light filled the air as I made my way out to the barn. Though I'd long lost sight of my feet as my growing stomach rounded out in front of me, and I felt a little more tired these days, I found the new morning after a restless night invigorating. The smell of dewy grass tingled my nose and bare feet.

Bessie, a camel-colored Jersey cow with a lop-sided white star on her forehead, mooed softly to greet me when I entered the barn. Her udders were full and ready to be milked. As I poured a bucket of feed into the trough, I petted her fuzzy shoulder. The smell of manure mixed with fresh hay filled the barn with a smell so familiar that I barely noticed it.

I eased myself onto the milking stool and put the bucket in front of my rounded belly, under Bessie's udder. A bit of milk dripped from one teat the moment I placed my fingers on it. She was ready to give me a full bucket. I squeezed and pulled the teats with both hands in turn as the satisfying streams of milk sprang forth with a sing-song sound into the stainless steel bucket.

Right in the middle of milking, a strong contraction squeezed my uterus, making me catch my breath. I paused as it held on, breathing through the contraction. Once it passed, I went back to milking. Minutes later, another contraction gripped me. I paused and breathed again, leaning against Bessie's warm fuzzy side this time. That was a strong one.

Was it the real thing? Was my labor starting? I finished milking in between a couple more contractions and made my way back to the house to tell Samuel that I might be going into labor.

Samuel went to the neighbor's house to use their phone to call our midwife, Tiva Baker, a local *Englisha* midwife. She was a natural herbalist from a

long line of American Indian healers, and her presence calmed me from the moment I first met her. I
liked Tiva.

When he called, she told him that she was attending another birth but he should keep in touch,
and she would get to our house in plenty of time for
our birth.

———————

Just three months earlier, we had been living
in Kentucky. Samuel was true to his word, and we left
New York soon after I got back from my trip to Michigan with my family. We left without telling anyone,
except Samuel's mom. The Mennonite preacher and
his wife had picked us up, along with a few boxes, and
brought us there. When I got there, I wrote a letter to
my parents, telling them of the move and where we
had moved to.

The preacher and his wife were really kind
people, and they introduced us to a group of other Mennonites, several of whom had also left the
Amish. They still dressed plain, in long dark clothes
that looked similar to the Amish clothing that we

were used to wearing, with the exception that Mennonite dresses were allowed to have zippers. But the men wore pants they had purchased instead of homemade *lots hussa*, with store-bought button-up shirts. I soon made a new friend, and she helped me sew some Mennonite dresses and adjust to the new life that I'd been thrust into.

Everything was new and different. We moved into a small house with electricity and indoor plumbing. That part of our new life was wonderful. The Mennonites from the church brought groceries for us and dropped them off in a large laundry basket, relieving my fear of spending too much money to restock our new home with food.

Samuel decided that it was time for him to learn how to drive so we could get our own car. And so he practiced until he passed his driving test and got his license. The idea of having our own car and being able to go somewhere without calling an *Englisha* driver was such a foreign idea to me, and it was exciting.

Samuel got a good deal on a worn Ford Escort Wagon. The day after he bought it, he got black spray paint and taped up the windows of the car to paint it black. In the Mennonite church, everyone painted their cars black. Other colors were not allowed.

At first, the car and all the technology was exciting. But soon the newness wore off, and I spent my days sitting and staring out of the living room window, missing my sisters. Not only had we moved away from my family, but we left the only life I knew. We were now excommunicated from the Amish, and I was only eighteen years old, newly married, and pregnant.

Up until now, I'd never imagined such a change in my life as this one. I was died-in-the-wool Amish. I kept nearly every Amish rule and ordinance because I wanted what was right with my whole heart. I wanted to please *Gott in Himmel.* I wanted to be good enough for a chance to make it into heaven someday. Now I'd been rudely and suddenly torn away from my family and eternally separated from the religion of my upbringing. I was scared that I was doomed, forever.

Still, I tried to be hopeful, even though I was very lonely and cried at night after Samuel fell asleep, holding my growing pregnant middle. Samuel rode to work every day with several other Mennonite men.

He came home exhausted each evening and fell asleep right after dinner. I felt like the loneliness of my life might swallow me whole, and I found myself wishing that it would.

———

Samuel took me to see a doctor. Even though the doctor was a man, he made me feel at ease right away. Our baby's heartbeat sounded healthy and everything looked good to Doctor Howard. I felt grateful that he would be the one to deliver our baby. While we decided to wait until the baby was born to find out its sex, I felt sure that I was carrying a baby girl.

A few weeks later, I got a letter in the mail, and my heart started racing when I recognized my mom's handwriting. When I opened the envelope, I found letters from both my parents. Their letters were kind and informational, with an update on their lives and their hope that I was doing well. I wrote back immediately and thanked them for writing. After that, I got a new letter every week.

Since Samuel and I were excommunicated,

we were also shunned, which meant my parents technically weren't allowed to write to me, but they did anyway. Each time I opened up a new letter from my family, I felt less alone and less afraid.

Two months before I was due to have our baby, Samuel told me that we were going to move back to New York for a little while. His family had decided to sell their farm and move to a new settlement in Ghent, Kentucky, a new Mennonite community where most of Samuel's family had just moved to, about two hours away from our Mennonite community. Before Samuel's parents could move, they needed to get their farm ready to sell, so we were moving back to New York to help them.

A range of mixed emotions filled my mind as I thought about going back to New York. We were excommunicated now, along with Samuel's parents. I missed my family in ways I couldn't describe, and it would be torturous to be so close to my family yet not able to go to their house. The rules of the *Shunning* kept me away from my loved ones. Oh, it all felt so cruel.

When I asked Samuel where I would have our baby, he replied that we'd have our baby at his parent's home, with a midwife.

What? My mom had all of her children at the hospital. Samuel and I had agreed to have our baby at the local hospital, in Kentucky, with Doctor Howard. But now he'd changed his mind again, without discussing it with me. It was my pregnant body, and yet it seemed like I wouldn't have a choice about how I brought this baby into the world.

Soon after we moved back to New York, Tiva Baker showed up at our house for the first house visit to check up on my pregnancy. Just like Doctor Howard, she made me feel comfortable and at ease. She was a veteran when it came to delivering babies at home, so I tried not to worry about my approaching due date, which was just two months away.

One month before my due date, we were on the road again. This time, we were headed to Missouri in our black Ford Escort Wagon. Samuel had received a call from his cousin, saying he was troubled and thinking about leaving the Amish, so Samuel promised that we would come out to Missouri to talk to him, and he would be welcome to come home with us as well.

It seemed like we would never get there. Being about eight months pregnant and riding in a car for days was certainly not my idea of fun. When nightfall came, we didn't stop for a hotel. Instead, we tried to get some sleep in the back of our wagon.

I couldn't sleep, the sound of traffic and the cool spring air keeping me awake on the stiff surface of the back car seat. No matter which way I turned, I couldn't find a comfortable position. Samuel passed out and slept for a couple hours before waking up refreshed and ready to hit the road again.

We finally got to where his cousin was staying, which was a bad area of the city. His cousin had already left the Amish to stay with some *Englisha* friends. There were drunks and druggies everywhere, and I did not feel safe at all. Samuel tried talking to his cousin, but he did not want to leave after all.

How ridiculous to have driven all this way for nothing, I thought. It would have been better and cheaper for us to have bought the cousin a bus ticket.

Without having time to shower and still feeling tired after our long trip, I got back into the car and headed back to New York. On the way home, the old wagon broke down. We had to get it towed off the interstate, and Samuel made some phone calls.

Since we were only about an hour or two away from the small Mennonite church we had attended in Kentucky just a month earlier, one of the members agreed to come and pick us up. It was like a miracle for my tired body and mind. We stayed at their house for a few days while our car was being fixed.

Though Samuel was so upset about the car breaking down and growing more sullen as the days went by, I was grateful to be around kind people with a warm shower for a few days.

Trying to ease Samuel's mood, I said to him, "Isn't it normal for vehicles to break down? It's not if, but when. I'm just glad we are able to stay with the Millers while our car is fixed. It could be so much worse for us than this."

Well, as I was still learning, Samuel got so angry when he had to spend any money. He did not agree with my viewpoint, nor did he like my remark, and he let me know it. Once the car was fixed, he picked it up, and we rode the rest of the way to his parent's home in utter silence.

As soon as we pulled into the driveway, Samuel practically jumped from the car and ran inside. By the time I got my large pregnant self out of the car and waddled into the house, I found him sitting on the floor in front of his mom.

He had his head in her lap. She was stroking his hair while he cried and told her how much it cost to fix our car. Samuel's mom was speaking to him like he was a little child as she comforted him. He was a twenty-eight-year-old grown man. *Or is he really grown? What kind of man acts this way?* I said nothing to either of them as I made my way around them and carried our luggage to our part of the house.

The rest of the month flew by, and the morning of my due date arrived.

After Samuel called Tiva Baker, my contractions continued at a regular pace. I didn't want to sit around, doing nothing during labor, so I began cleaning the house. My nesting instinct had kicked into full force. I dusted, swept, and mopped the entire house, and washed all the windows.

Tiva arrived sometime in the early afternoon. When she hugged me and touched my stomach, my body seemed to receive a message that it was safe to go into full labor, and my water broke. Then, what had felt like manageable contractions up until that point, suddenly felt unbearable. I gasped from the pain.

My gentle midwife sensed that transition wasn't too far away, so she went to the kitchen to heat up some water on the wood-burning stove in our kitchen. While she was away from my side, another contraction gripped my body with its iron teeth, sucking my breath away. I got up after it passed, panicking from the intensity of the pain.

I can't do this, I thought. *I have to get away. I can't. I can't. I can't.*

Any logical reasoning had made itself scarce as my urge to escape this process took over, and I took off running. I flew past Tiva in the kitchen, out the front door, and down the road. I wanted to run away from the pain. I wanted to run away from everything that had come with my marriage to Samuel.

Samuel caught up to me first, with Tiva not far behind him, and together they brought me back to the house. Tiva wasn't rattled by my runaway act. Instead, she soothed me and coached me through the next contractions that came.

When she checked me and saw I was ready to transition, she sanitized one of my big Amish bowls and filled it with warm water. She sent Samuel to get a few other things before she turned and focused her attention on me.

Her calm strength steadied me through another difficult contraction, then another one right on the heels of it. One right after another.

"It's time, Anna."

I panted. "I have to push."

"Yes, push."

I squeezed her arm and let out a loud moan as I pushed. Moments later a baby was born, screaming. Tiva moved quickly yet calmly. As soon as she cut the cord, Tiva carefully submerged the baby into a giant bowl of warm water where it immediately calmed down and quit crying.

"Anna, you have a sweet little baby girl." Tiva smiled up at me from the warm bowl of water where she was still holding my baby.

I lay there as a surreal feeling washed over me

and tears ran down my face. I could not believe I had a beautiful baby girl!

She was a world of wonder to breathe in. I touched her head full of black hair, admiring her perfect face with a tiny button nose. She had every toe and every finger. Her ears were tiny and perfect. She was perfect in every way and the most beautiful baby I had ever seen.

When Tiva laid her on my chest, she snuggled into my skin. Mother and daughter, content and complete with one another, connected to an infinity that stretched beyond us.

"What will we name her?" I whispered to Samuel.

He'd been standing there, speechless, taking it all in. Now he eased onto the bed beside me and admired our perfect little girl with me.

"Do you want to hold her?" I asked him another question. It felt safe to ask him anything that I wanted to ask in this sacred, quiet space.

He chuckled nervously. "It's okay; you just keep her for now."

I didn't know that he'd never held a newborn baby before. A few minutes later he changed his mind, though, and Tiva took our baby from me and laid her in his arms, careful to support her tiny head. I watched the feeling of awe and wonder wash over his face as he held our precious baby in his arms.

Long rays from the afternoon sun lowered themselves gently across the wooden floor and touched the bed, polishing our skin with a golden glow. We were now a family of three.

While I was still pregnant, we'd talked about the boys' and girls' names that we both liked, but we couldn't settle on one. Now Samuel wrote down all the girl names we had chosen and put them into his wide-brimmed, black Amish church hat.

Laura, Elizabeth, Rhoda, Anna, Margaret, Rachel—the white slips of paper swirled and bounced. He reached into the hat, his fingers closing around one of those random white pieces. He pulled out the paper and opened it. The providence of our firstborn's name was revealed: Anna.

Soon it was time for everyone else to meet little Anna. Samuel's mom came over to hold her and gush over the baby. The next day my parents secretly pulled in with their horse and buggy to see their new granddaughter.

When Mom asked Samuel if the baby and I could come stay with them for a week so she could help to take care of us, I held my breath. Oh, how I wanted that. It didn't take much of a convincing effort, though. Samuel was a proud dad, and he was happy to make me happy. He said yes, and so I was allowed to take baby Anna and go home with my parents.

The Amish church did not approve of my parents helping us, since we were excommunicated. No one said anything about it to me, but I knew that my parents were bending the rules to have my baby and me in their home. Perhaps the natural act of caring for a young mother and her baby trumped the church's rules, so the bishop looked the other way.

It was such an honor to have Mom's help during the first week of being a new mom. She taught me how to bathe and breastfeed baby Anna before sending me to my old room to get more sleep.

"Soon you'll get your energy back and you'll feel like doing things, but you mustn't," Mom said.

"If you don't rest enough, you'll get behind on sleep for months to come."

Each day felt like a precious treasure. Breast-feeding. Snuggling. Sleeping. On repeat. Nothing else mattered.

———————

I went back home to Samuel when baby Anna was one week old. It was in the afternoon. His parents had already left to go on a trip to Kentucky. As soon as we got into the house with the baby, Samuel started taking my clothes off.

Nervous, I tried to stop him. "Samuel, the baby is only a week old. We have to wait for six weeks for my body to heal before we have sex."

He wasn't stopping. "Your body belongs to me, and I want it now." He kissed me forcefully as I turned my face.

"Please don't, Samuel, please let's wait," I pleaded, but he didn't listen.

Stilling my desire to resist him, I wordlessly submitted myself under my husband as he relieved himself. It hurt physically, but the emotional pain was

much worse. I felt the tears coming as I closed my
eyes and mentally escaped my body.

6.

A Son Is Born

Spring 1989

Samuel had decided that it was time to move back to Kentucky when baby Anna was only four months old. We moved to a new conservative Mennonite settlement in the small southern town of Ghent, Kentucky, nestled in deep green hollers along the south bank of the Ohio River.

Little Anna, now a toddler, was napping when I carefully snuck out of the house to go work in the garden. Samuel had plowed an acre of ground for me to plant and grow vegetables for the year.

In the early spring months of the year, I'd hoed long, even rows in the dirt to plant seeds. First, I planted peas, lettuce, radishes, and cabbage seeds.

These were our spring crops. I was pleased to see plump pods full of peas hanging from tender stalks, and I plucked enough to shell and steam for dinner.

During the warm months of the year, we ate primarily from the garden. I collected mason jars to preserve the extra produce that would sustain us during the winter months. One week, our neighbor gave us a box of jars, and it felt like a precious gift.

Before I put little Anna down for a nap, I'd washed all the jars and set them out on towels on the kitchen table to dry. Feeling satisfied as they glistened crisp and clean, I envisioned them stuffed full of vegetables, fruit, and meat, lined up on shelves in the pantry of our new home that Samuel was building.

Now it was time to plant tomatoes, green beans, cucumbers, and corn. If I worked quickly, I could get a lot done before little Anna woke up. I was eight months pregnant, and the baby inside of me slept as my body rocked back and forth, swinging the hoe in the spring sunshine.

When I straightened my back, I remembered to go check on my sleeping toddler. I made my way from the garden to the shed that was our temporary home. It looked cute, set amongst the trees along a wide creek. I felt like Laura Ingalls again, living like a pioneer woman.

I opened the door of the shed to find two-year-old Anna standing in a circle of broken glass beside the table full of mason jars. My mouth went dry.

"*Vas is des!*" I heard myself shriek.

Little Anna must have crawled out of bed to find her small blue sippy cup, which had been left on the table beside the rows of freshly washed mason jars. When she reached for it, she had knocked down several jars, and they shattered instantly on the concrete floor.

My fear switched from shock to anger. I don't remember what I said to her, but she quickly understood that she was in trouble. She listened to my urgent instructions to stand completely still until I cleaned up a path through the broken glass to snatch her up.

I carried her outside, carefully inspecting her fingers and toes in the bright sunlight. There was nothing. Not a single cut. She was completely unharmed by the glass.

Trembling, I hugged her tight, grateful that she was alright, my tears mingling with hers.

———————

Most of Samuel's family had moved to the community, along with my older brother and one of my sisters and their families. Each of us had left the Amish, and we had decided to start a new church together.

Samuel used the cash in his savings account to buy and split a hundred acres of land with his dad and another member of our church. A creek ran through our half of the property, so Samuel built a bridge over the creek and started building a house for us up on the side of the steep hill that the locals called a holler.

While he built the house, we lived in a shed with a concrete floor. Now it was two years later and we were still living in the shed, but he promised that the house would be done before this baby was born.

When I wasn't tending to the garden or washing laundry, I visited with the ladies in our community. Sometimes we helped each other with garden work or housework or sewing clothes, and discussed all the gossip as we worked together. I always heard about the strife amongst the men in the community. Everyone seemed to have a different idea of how the church should be, and no one could agree on what the new set of rules would be.

I didn't understand it at all. So much of our new church's teaching was still based on outward performance. To me, it felt like there were more rules and regulations than what I had grown up within the Amish church. While they preached a new type of teaching that stated we could believe in Jesus to be saved, our own good works were still required. It seemed the same as the Amish, to me. We had to confess each and every sin we had ever committed in order to receive a pardon, but the guilt for those sins always remained.

In my mind, God was still taking the form of being a fearsome, angry *Gott in Himmel* who saw everything I ever did and would punish me for each sin. I worried that I might have forgotten a sin and not confessed it. If I didn't confess and repent, then *Gott in Himmel* would never forgive me.

My understanding of *Gott in Himmel* was reinforced at home, where Samuel always pointed out my flaws and asked me why I couldn't be more like other women? I was never enough. I never measured up to the standard that I needed to meet for Samuel or *Gott in Himmel.* My inability to live up to *Gott in Himmel* and Samuel's standards produced a dark cloud that hung over my consciousness.

Still, I tried my best to be a happy and obedient wife. I began to pray every day that *Gott in Himmel* would break me and make me like the woman that Samuel thought I should be like. I prayed for forgiveness and wanted so much to believe that *Gott in Himmel* was hearing my prayers.

Mark was born on a Saturday morning in the basement of our new Kentucky home. Samuel had kept his promise. The house wasn't finished, but it had a roof and walls and plumbing, so we could live in the basement until the upstairs was ready to live in.

During my long labor, the baby's heart rate went way down. My Mennonite midwife was concerned that something could be wrong, so we made a trip to the hospital. They hooked me up to different machines and checked me out. Everything seemed to be okay, and by then, the baby's heart rate had gone back up. I was so relieved. So we went back home, and baby Mark was born several hours later. He was just as cute and perfect as Anna. In fact, he looked just like her with a head full of soft black hair and big, soulful eyes.

We should have been the perfect happy family with two cute children. But times were tough. Samuel said that money was tight because he had built us a new house. Always unhappy, he again talked about ending his life.

He said that, because of how I acted, he wanted to hang himself. I didn't know what I was doing wrong, so I prayed to *Gott in Himmel* to make me a better wife.

With feeling like a failure as a wife, I found all my joy in being a mom. I loved nursing and caring for Mark and little Anna. As I rocked them and sang to them, I felt a great strength rising inside of me. I knew that I would do anything to protect them.

The children loved me unconditionally, which was something I'd always longed for. I never felt rejected or not good enough for them, even though I wasn't a perfect mom.

When Mark was thirteen months old, I got pregnant again, and I immediately felt that it was a boy. I was about seven months pregnant when the children and I went to Michigan with my older brother to visit my parents, who had moved there.

On the way home, I bought some canned baby food to feed Mark because I was no longer producing enough breast milk to keep him satisfied. By the time we got home, he was throwing up.

Mark continued throwing up all night. The next day, I convinced Samuel that I needed to take baby Mark to a local family doctor. He gave me some suppositories that were supposed to stop the baby from throwing up, but it didn't work. He just continued throwing up.

He wanted water so bad, so I'd give him just a little, but he just couldn't keep it down. This continued on into the next night. He looked so frail, and his lips turned blue every time his small body heaved, no longer having anything left to throw up. I could hardly stand it. My tiny son was so sick, and I was afraid he would die. I started crying, begging Samuel to help me.

Finally, he took both of us to the emergency room. I showed the nurse what the doctor had given me as they checked him out, and they said I needed to keep putting in the suppositories. They said they couldn't do anything more for him and sent us home.

By the next morning, I was about beside myself with worry because my baby wasn't getting better. My intuition was telling me the baby food that I'd fed him had been spoiled, and he had a bad case of food poisoning.

Worn out from continual dry heaving and still unable to keep anything down, he lay down on the bare, concrete floor. He looked so thin, and his lips were blue. His eyes were rolling back into his head. I knelt beside him, weeping.

I cried out to *Gott in Himmel.* "Oh, God, I can hardly stand to see my little son like this. He is suffering so much. Please, God, if it is your will, please heal him. God, if he is not going to grow up to serve you, then just take him home to you now. Please, God, I want Mark to be a man of God. Oh please heal him."

I collapsed into tears on the floor beside my baby. Exhausted because I hadn't slept in days, I had nothing left inside of me. I was so scared of losing my baby, and I was afraid if I fell asleep, he would die. I sat up and pulled him close against my large pregnant middle, even though I hardly had a lap left to hold him. My tears fell on his head as I waited for something to happen.

"Mom," he whimpered in a tone that was barely audible. *"Ich vill ein getrank."*

He was asking for a drink, and I gave it to him, believing he would throw it up again. It all just seemed so endless. It felt like a nightmare. *But wait!* Several minutes passed, and he didn't throw up. Several more minutes passed. Still, my son was keeping this liquid in his body. *Could I hope that he would live?*

He lay quietly on my lap, a peaceful look on his small face. He asked for another drink, and I gave it to him. Again, the minutes ticked by without the liquid coming back up.

Oh, Gott in Himmel. Did you heal my little boy?

I hardly dared to breathe! A few moments later, he asked for a Popsicle. Trembling from a combination of exhaustion mixed with hope, I went to the freezer and pulled out a cheap plastic tube with a frozen Kool-Aid mixture. He licked and nibbled the

Popsicle for a bit before handing it back to me.

We lay down on the couch together, curled up close so I could warm his cold body. Through blurry eyes, I watched his breathing as he fell asleep. I thanked *Gott in Himmel* as I, too, fell asleep. I felt a sense of peace deep in my heart as I knew *Gott in Himmel* had saved Mark from death. No longer just the unforgiving God, *Gott in Himmel* had done something merciful for both of us.

———

David was born in our basement home three weeks later. He looked a little different than little Anna and Mark. He was my smallest baby, fair-skinned with a head full of blond hair and blue eyes. He was tiny and perfect from his head to his itty bitty toes. Anna wanted to rock her baby brother and play with him.

Now I had three beautiful perfect kids, and they were my only happiness. I lived for them. Two years passed by, and baby David grew into a mischievous, tow-headed toddler. Everyone adored him.

One day, I left all of the children at my friend's

house so I could help Samuel's parents pick berries for a few hours. Their produce business was booming, and they needed extra hands to harvest the fruit.

When I got back to my friend's house a few hours later, David didn't come running when I called the children. My friend helped me search, but he was nowhere to be found. Panicking, we kept calling out his name. The world started spinning around me as I faced my worst nightmare.

Everyone joined the search party, running up and down the long driveway and through the bordering woods, calling out for David. Each moment felt like an eternity.

After thoroughly searching around my friend's house and property, we made our way over to her sister's house to ask her to help us look for the missing boy. And there he was! I ran over and scooped him up, holding him close, and wept.

I got pregnant again and Sammy, named after his father, was born in the fall of 1994. We were still living in the basement of our Kentucky home, and with each birth, I seemed to bleed more heavily. This time, my Mennonite midwife brought a new assistant with her that she had in training.

When Sammy was born, the midwife told her assistant that she could take the baby and clean him. But before the midwife had time to cut the cord, she picked baby Samuel up and started walking away. The cord still wasn't cut, so it began yanking inside of me.

My midwife panicked, which made me panic as well. Of course, the assistant felt awful for her mistake. In pain, I looked down to see heavy bleeding. Together they worked to try to stop my bleeding. They instructed Samuel to heat water for tea, and I drank as much of the strong cinnamon tea as I could, nearly gagging as I tried to gulp it down.

Finally the bleeding quit, and I was thankful to hold my beautiful new son in my arms. I marveled over his perfect features. My fourth child was born with a full head of light hair with a tint of red in it. I stroked it as I nursed him and he fell asleep.

The midwife thought I was doing okay, so she and her assistant both left. I felt weak and ready to fall asleep, grateful that I'd brought another baby safely into this world.

Before I could fall asleep, Samuel came into our bedroom and began pulling the blankets off, pushed the bloody pad away and got on top of me. I tried to resist him, but I was too weak. I just lay there and wept as he relieved himself into my torn, aching body.

———————

Samuel built a barn beside our unfinished house on the hill, and we added a small herd of animals to our growing family—pigs, goats, chickens, a pair of rabbits, and a dog.

At seven-years-old and four-years-old, little Anna and Mark were now old enough to collect the chicken eggs, take slop to the pigs, and feed the rabbits. By fall, the pigs would be fattened up, ready to butcher, and put away for our winter's food supply.

The days were long, but the weeks flew by as I mothered my young flock. I cooked, cleaned, sewed clothing for our family, gardened, canned food, homeschooled, and bathed the kids. I'd also begun piecing and quilting large bedspreads to sell and help bring in a little extra income for our family.

On a warm summer day, I chased the children out of the house to go play so I could get some sewing done. While they were playing, the older children convinced Davie, who was just a toddler, that goat turds were M&Ms. He came into the house a little while later, for a drink of water, with a dark brown ring around his mouth from eating goat poop.

I took him back outside with a clean face, scolded Mark and Anna for feeding their brother poop, and turned around to find Baby Sammy eating the dog food on the porch. I hoped that dog food and poop wouldn't hurt my children's digestive systems as I went back to my sewing.

Every Monday was laundry day. I gathered up all of our clothes while I heated a large kettle of water on the stove. I sorted the clothes into piles by color, making sure to separate all the whites. Little Anna helped me. The first load of clothes would be all of our whites, washed in the ringer washer on our front porch in the boiling water I'd heated. I added bleach to the water to brighten the whites and hung them out to dry on the line where they'd be further bleached by the bright morning sun.

After washing the rest of the clothing in another batch of warm water, I let the children help me ring out the clothes, keeping their little fingers away from the hand rollers. All it took was one time for one of them to yell from the pain of a smashed finger, and I no longer had to warn them to be careful.

Our dog got pregnant from the nightly visits of several neighborhood mutts and gave birth to a variety of different puppies. Now we were officially true-to-the-bone Kentucky hillbillies with a slew of odd-looking little puppies tumbling around our place. It took a lot of food to feed them, though, and that cost money.

Early one Sunday morning, after a week of rain, Samuel came into the house with a triumphant look on his face. "No more mutts running around here." His voice boomed through our tiny basement quarters.

Little Anna and Mark came running and peeked around my skirt, all of us looking at him.

"Gone with one swell of a wave." He slapped his knee and laughed.

"What do you mean, Samuel?"

"I put that whole litter of puppies in a gunny sack and flushed 'em down the creek. They were gone with one swell of a wave." He laughed again, but he was the only one laughing.

After that, he took out his shotgun and fired at any dogs that came onto our property to keep them away from our dog.

"No more mutts," he said. "No more."

Little Anna cried over the dead puppies, but she didn't dare let her dad see her tears.

Samuel killed one of our goats and butchered it because we had company coming, all the way from Florida, to our basement home. I had planned to butcher some chickens to feed our guests, but he told me that *Englisha* people liked eating burgers. So burgers they would have—goat burgers.

The family that was on their way to visit us were not exactly *Englisha* anymore since they had decided to leave their worldly career path and lead a plain lifestyle. Samuel and I had first met them on a trip with a Mennonite friend of ours, Levi Mast.

This family's last name, Leibee, was not an Amish name at all, so they were automatically marked as not truly being one of us. In our minds, you could only be Amish or Mennonite if you were born that way. It had to be in your blood, from the Anabaptist bloodline.

They had a big family, with adopted children from different races. I was completely fascinated by their family as they filed into our small house, one by one. I knew they might not be used to seeing a family that lived so simply. My cabinets had little curtains that hung over them instead of doors, and one side of my kitchen was lined with shelves full of canned goods. Our home was completely different from a typical *Englisha* home, that I knew.

Helen, the mom, struck up a conversation with me as I sliced a loaf of fresh bread for lunch. I told her that Samuel was working on finishing the upstairs of our house so we could live up there, suddenly feeling embarrassed by our simple dwelling. I offered her a kitchen chair to sit down, since the men were sitting on our single couch, and there was nowhere else to sit.

When she spoke to my children, who were watching shyly from the corner, they couldn't answer her. I translated, so they would understand what she was saying to them.

"They don't speak English yet," I tried to explain.

Pennsylvania Dutch was my children's first language, and the only way I spoke to my children. Since I homeschooled them, they hadn't yet been exposed to outsiders who spoke a different language.

Helen didn't understand, though. "How on earth do you homeschool them that way?" She didn't know that everything we did was different from her family's way of doing things, even though they were trying to lead plain lives.

I blushed and shrugged. I didn't know how to explain our ways to an outsider.

Soon lunch was ready to be served: Goat burgers. Potato salad. Steamed peas. Freshly washed lettuce leaves and sliced tomatoes from our garden to put on their goat burger sandwiches with homemade bread. And a chocolate cake with sliced peaches for dessert.

I was surprised when the man of the family didn't eat first, but instead helped his wife fix plates for their children and then made his own plate last.

After lunch, the children ran outside to play

while the grownups sat around and talked. Mostly I listened to the men and answered Helen's questions. I noticed the kind way that her husband spoke to her and looked at her. I decided that I really liked this *Englisha* plain family. They seemed like good people.

A year after Sammy was born, I had a miscarriage. I was only two months pregnant, but I still felt the loss of a tiny soul. I secretly named the baby Christy, a non-Amish name, after the main character in a historical fiction novel by Catherine Marshall.

In the afternoons, while the children were taking their naps, I made time to curl up and read for a while. I could relate to Christy's journey into the Appalachian Mountains to teach school and navigating how to live in primitive conditions while nurturing the students she grew to love.

Since Samuel's parents lived just over the holler from us, I took the children there for the day so I could get some sewing done and, hopefully, get some time to read my book.

The children loved their grandparents. They lived in a fully finished house, surrounded by acres of gardens and a large orchard. Below the orchard was a large pond with a fishing dock, stocked with fish and big enough to go boating on. Samuel's dad, who we all called Grosdawdy, ran a thriving produce business, irrigating the produce with water from the pond. When Grosmommy wasn't helping him pick berries, she made jam and quilted quilts to sell.

One of the children's favorite pastimes at Grosdawdy and Grosmommy's house was to play by a hole in the upstairs floor, which created a vent for the heat from the wood cooking stove to go upstairs. In the wintertime, the upstairs was heated through the hole. An iron grate covered the hole so that nothing big would fall through it. Grosmommy always pretended like she didn't hear the children when they watched her through the grate.

Sometimes they lifted the iron grate up out of the floor and threaded their fabric ropes down through it to send down to a sibling or cousin who would wait for it downstairs. Since the hole was big enough for one of the small children to fall through it, when Grosmommy found them playing around the hole with the iron grate removed, they'd get a scolding.

Sometimes the children got even more creative with their games. They loved to drop their popcorn through the hole to see if they could hit someone that was walking by down below. Their older cousin Jerry would squeal and yell at them in Pennsylvania Dutch, with threats to find them and tickle them. Giggling, the children would scamper away.

That day when I pulled into the driveway to pick up the children, I knew something was wrong because everyone was gathering around a child on the ground. I don't know how it happened, but Sammy had gotten hurt. Grosdawdy picked him up and carried him into the house with a nasty-looking head wound. I hurried after him, surrounded by a small crowd of my nieces and nephews.

I wrung my hands as I got closer to my son. It looked like the skin of his scalp had been peeled back. There was so much blood. I felt queasy.

"Shouldn't we take him to the hospital?" I asked, wondering what my husband's father was going to do with my small son.

Grosdawdy ignored me and demanded that someone go and get his bottle of Listerine. One of my nieces scampered off to go get it.

I doubted he knew the right way to handle this injury. However, a woman shouldn't question a man's judgment—still, I wanted to grab my son and take him to the hospital.

"*Bish to sure* you should put Listerine on it?" I asked. "Don't you think it needs stitches?

"Oh *yah*, this is the best thing for it." Grosdawdy finally acknowledged me. "Here, help hold him."

I did as I was told. Grosdawdy took a cap full of Listerine and started pouring it over Sammy's open head wound. Sammy screamed while I tried to hold him still, assuring him, despite my own doubts, that he was going to be alright.

"Some tape'll fix 'im up," Grosdawdy grunted.

Grosmommy got the scissors from one of her kitchen drawers to cut the hair around Sammy's wound. Through it all, Sammy kept screaming, his face pinched in agony, his eyes wild and afraid. Unfazed by the blood or the screaming, Grosdawdy kept working to clean and patch up his head.

Later, Mark and David told me that they had all taken a dare to jump off a stack of pallets. Sammy was only two years old, but he wanted to jump too. He wanted to be one of the big boys. When he jumped, a broken board caught the back of his head, tearing it open. Sammy's head healed after some time, leaving a large, jagged scar on the crown of his head.

———————

I conceived again, and another son joined our growing family, late in the month of May. The basement was much nicer now and not as dark. Samuel had enclosed part of the porch, giving us a more spacious living room. Though we needed more space with our growing family, we didn't have enough money to finish the upstairs. I helped Samuel paint the concrete floor, adding a patterned texture with a sponge.

For this birth, we set up a twin bed in the living room. Baby Mose was born with a head full of blond hair and big blue eyes. He was my biggest baby and my scariest birth.

After the midwife laid my newborn son on

my chest, she exclaimed over the amount of blood that was draining from my body. She and her helper started using different methods to stop the bleeding: coaxing me to drink a strong herbal tea and vigorously massaging my stomach to help the uterus contract, which would stop the bleeding. None of their efforts were working.

Feeling weaker as I listened to the concerned conversation between the midwife and her helper, my eyes grew heavy, but I fought to stay awake. Through the fussy haze settled around me, one comment stood out to me: my midwife was getting ready to call 911.

Drifting in and out of consciousness, my life began flashing before my eyes, taking me back to my last conversation with my dad only a year earlier. I could see his face so clearly, framed by his snowy white hair and beard. With unclouded eyes gazing steadily into mine, he held my hand as he told me he loved me. I squeezed his hands hard as we shed some happy tears. A few hours later, I stood by his bedside with my siblings as he took his final breath.

Now I felt that I would be joining my dad in heaven, and I felt a sense of peace washing over me. As I lay there tenderly holding my newborn son, I no longer wanted to fight to stay awake.

The midwife and her helper were still working to stop the hemorrhaging on their own. Finally, the crisis was averted when the flow of bleeding slowed down, and they were able to stabilize me. We lived a long way from the hospital, so it would have taken an ambulance a while to get to me. Again, *Gott in Himmel* was merciful and spared my life.

Shakily, the midwife sat down beside me to monitor me.

"Anna, a good long break before another pregnancy would be wise," she said after a while. "Your body is simply worn out from having so many babies."

My mind was tired, but I tried to follow what my midwife was saying.

She continued on, carefully. "Maybe just think about getting your tubes tied. I don't know what will happen if you have another baby, and I worry about you."

I nodded because I understood. As much I loved each of my children, I didn't want to think of going through another frightening birth experience.

She stayed with me for the rest of the night to

keep an eye on me. I was secretly thankful. I couldn't bear the thought of Samuel having sex with me again so soon after giving birth. I wondered how much time I had before I would get pregnant again, and then I put those thoughts aside and fell asleep.

———

A few weeks went by before I finally got up enough nerve to speak to Samuel about the break that my body needed from having babies. It seemed like he was in a good mood when I brought it up to him.

"Sam"—I stroked his back just the way he liked—"the midwife told me I could have died when Baby Mose was born because my body is worn out. I bled so much." I paused.

He nodded, and that encouraged me to keep talking.

"We have a beautiful family with five healthy children. I love all of them." I paused again.

I could see his cheeks move as he smiled and reached up to squeeze my hand. My heart started beating faster now.

"I'm so afraid about what might happen if I

have another baby, with all the bleeding . . ." My voice trailed off. And then I gathered every ounce of bravery I had, my voice barely more than a whisper. "Do you think that I could go in and get my tubes tied?" I nervously let that loaded question hang in the air by itself and wiped away a brave little tear that squeezed from the corner of my eye before Samuel could see it, steadying my shaking hands.

To my surprise, Samuel agreed. I could go in and get my tubes tied. We would be done having children. So I called and made an appointment.

The day before my scheduled appointment, Samuel changed his mind, saying it was against the word of *Gott in Himmel,* and we'd just have to trust that I wouldn't die while giving birth in the future. When he saw the devastation on my face, he told me that I didn't have any faith in God.

All I wanted to know was, how could my husband so easily break his promise to me and then use the Word of God to make himself look good and to make me look like the evil one? That just didn't seem right.

For the life of me, I can't remember what he did wrong. But I know I was overwhelmed. I was stressed out. So when Sammy did whatever he did that day, it no longer mattered that he was only three years old. I was angry.

When he looked up and saw me coming at him with anger written all over my face, he took off running. That made me even angrier. When I got to him, I grabbed him roughly, throwing his squirming body across my lap and wailing on his backside. He screamed as I hit him harder. I couldn't stop beating him.

I released all of my resentment as I punished my young son for the minor offense he'd committed and it felt good in the moment, even justified. It was so wrong, though, and later the regret of my actions filled me with deep despair. My growing anger that bubbled just beneath the surface now made me afraid of myself.

Holding baby Anna | Norfolk, NY   *Sewing Clothes | Ghent, KY*

Little Anna, "Mark", and "David" | Ghent, KY

Our Kentucky Home

Little Anna and "Mark" with some of their cousins | Ghent, KY

A Family Photo | Ghent, Kentucky

Little Anna and I | *At my sister's house*

7.

On the Move, Again

Summer 1996

Life turned into a sequence of things that happened either with or without me, and I was just along for the ride. After nearly ten years of living in Kentucky, Samuel decided that we needed to move to a new Mennonite settlement in a state out west that I'd barely even heard of: Idaho. The idea of moving to Idaho felt like moving to a whole new country, and I felt like a pioneer as I began packing up our belongings to head west.

Samuel finally finished building the upstairs of our little Kentucky house so it would be ready to sell. I admired the newly finished drywall and flooring and looked out the windows to appreciate the view from up there, imagining what it would have been like to live upstairs.

An *Englisha* Realtor came out from the city to put up a fancy plastic sign along the road at the front of our property. When she asked the children how old they were, little Anna translated for her siblings. She understood a little English, enough to tell the younger ones what the smiling lady was asking them, before she proudly answered the lady with the numbers of their ages.

It took a few months for our Realtor to find a buyer for our little Kentucky house on fifty acres. And then, without a place lined up to live in when we got to Idaho, we put all of our belongings on a pull-behind trailer, pulled a tarp over it, and hit the road.

It took three days of driving to get to Grangeville, Idaho. I took turns driving when Samuel needed to get some sleep. When the children got hungry, we stopped to buy a loaf of bread, bologna, and pickles from a grocery store along the interstate. During the trip, I made sandwiches in the van for everyone. This was a treat for the children.

In Idaho, someone in our new community

knew about a small house in town that we could rent for a few months while we found something to live in permanently. It didn't take long for Samuel to buy and purchase seven acres of land just outside of town.

I helped him as much as I could as he built a new house for our family. This one didn't have a basement. We would live in a wide-open space above ground, with windows that looked out over the prairie amidst mountains rising to the west of our place.

Idaho was cold and empty and wild and beautiful. On Sunday afternoons, we went on long drives to explore the new state that we lived in. Every time we passed a fresh mountain spring coming out of the mountainside, Samuel pulled the van over to the side of the road and got the children out of the car so they could drink fresh, cold spring water.

When we discovered wild apple trees and berry bushes growing along the road, we drove home to get buckets and went back to pick as much fruit as we could. I made pie filling and jam with the fruit and canned it.

Though I had initially been skeptical, Idaho had its perks. Most importantly, Samuel seemed so much happier in this new place, and we were making new friends in our community.

Most of the members of our community were *Englisha* people who wanted to adopt plain ways of living. Some of the women asked me how to can food, and I was happy to teach them. I also learned so many new things from them.

While some things were better, making a living out west wasn't easy. With fewer people living in our area, Samuel had less work. The closest city with a Walmart was seventy-five miles away, and Samuel didn't want to drive to the city for work.

In the past, Samuel worked in construction, but here there weren't many building projects nor the budget for them. So he built a big shop on our place and started building storage sheds, gazebos, and lawn furniture. He put up a sign in our front yard, and the local *Englisha* began buying a few of the things he built. With our dwindling funds and lack of income, Samuel started to feel stressed.

One day, I was outside in the yard when I heard a horrible screaming sound coming from the shop. I dropped what I was doing and quickly ran out there. Just as I got to the door, I heard the sound of a large piece of wood hit the floor. I rounded the corner of the door to see Mark shaking all over. Samuel was standing over him.

"*Vas is letz?*" I asked, an awful sick feeling taking over my stomach.

I could not make myself even think that Samuel might have been hitting Mark with the long piece of 2" x 4" lumber that was lying on the floor next to his son. That board looked bigger than our small boy. But, yes, it was true. Samuel took his anger and stress out by beating Mark's small body with that piece of lumber.

In silence, because I didn't know what to say and because I was afraid of my husband, I went to Mark and picked him up. Samuel made a disgusted grunting sound and walked away. I didn't know what else to do but to comfort my young son.

The following week, Samuel created a chart that he put on the refrigerator.

"Anna, it's time the children learn how to obey us and be more responsible. 'Train up a child in the way he shall go.'" He quoted Bible verses as a weapon. "'Children, obey your parents in the Lord.'"

If this was what God said and how he meant it, then there was no questioning it.

No wrongdoing could go unpunished from now on. Each time a child didn't listen during the week, we placed a mark under their name. Every Monday morning, a reckoning would take place: Samuel gave each child a spanking for every mark on the chart. He made a new paddle in the shop from a piece of 1" x 4" lumber. He drilled holes in it to make sure the air couldn't cushion the blows of the paddle during a beating.

The children dreaded Monday mornings. Each time, they lined up to receive their spankings for everything they'd done wrong the week before. If they took their spankings without crying too much, they would be over with it quickly. Crying loudly was seen as a sign of rebellion and always incurred extra whacks from the paddle in order to beat it out of the child. Since the younger children didn't have the strength to keep from crying out, especially Sammy, they got longer spankings than the others.

On one such Monday morning, Sammy went into the bedroom to get his weekly reckoning. Samuel closed the door, and we listened as it started. Everyone was quiet as Sammy's cries and the sound of the paddle on his bare skin filled the room.

I closed my eyes, silently praying that it would all be over soon so we could get on with our week. But this time, it didn't stop.

The sounds of the beating got louder and Samuel started yelling at Sammy. "Settle down and take your spanking!"

Samuel called it a spanking, but it was a beating.

Sammy cried out in pain as the paddle hit his back, and Samuel laughed. "I've got all day, boy. I can do this all day." He welded the paddle with even more force and slammed it across Sammy's body, laughing hysterically. The sound of his laughter was evil, sending chills up my spine.

Suddenly, I saw Anna jump up. She'd had it. She couldn't take the sound of the beating anymore. She ran up the stairs into the room above Samuel. I'll never know how she did it, but she grabbed a giant chest of drawers and pushed it over. The sound of the dresser hitting the floor thundered throughout the house, and it made Samuel stop beating Sammy.

He burst out of the room with the paddle still in his hand, furious.

"What's going on," he asked me.

I said nothing to answer him, frozen in place. Before I could think, he was bounding up the stairs. *Is he going to kill Anna now?*

Anna faced her dad with a fearless look on her young face. "I want it to stop," she said to him, her slender body standing tall and strong. She didn't care if she took the beating in her brother's place. To my surprise, Samuel didn't touch her. He scolded her until she cried, and then he left the house.

Sammy lay listlessly around the house for the rest of that day and didn't act like his usual self during the next few days. That wasn't the last time Samuel beat the children, but for that day, it had stopped. Perhaps Anna saved her brother that day of dying from a beating.

It would have been unthinkable for me to leave my husband or report abuse. That thought didn't even cross my mind. I just blamed myself for what was happening in our home, and I felt terrified. My husband was a monster, and I didn't know that I could find a way out. Instead, I tried to find ways to be a better wife and soothe my husband.

I got pregnant again, and nine months and two weeks later, I brought a daughter safely into the world with the help of a new, local midwife. We named her Laura. Anna was on top of the world because she finally had a sister. Baby Laura had a head full of black hair. She was absolutely beautiful and perfect in every way.

Her gray eyes changed to a beautiful blue and green color and her thick, dark hair turned into golden ringlets by the time she was six months old. Laura was sweet and beautiful, and everyone adored her, especially her big sister. There was a special grace about her presence that brought peace into every room she toddled into.

Laura grew from a gentle and quiet baby to a sweet and thoughtful young girl. The only thing she ever begged for was for me to read stories to her. None of my other children loved stories as much as little Laura.

She also shared a special connection with Mose, and he loved to take care of her. I smiled as I watched them play together. When Laura fell, Mose always helped her get back up, putting his arm around her as they walked.

———————

At the end of 1999, just three years after we moved to Idaho, Samuel decided it was time to move again. His parents were getting older, and they needed our help. Moving to Idaho had cost us a lot more financially than he'd anticipated, and Samuel hoped that better work would be available in Michigan, where his parents were living.

We bought forty acres near southern Michigan and built a 5,000-square foot log home on it. It took over a year to place the logs and seal up the walls, so we lived in one end of a pole barn while we built the house.

Something about our experience of living in Idaho had caused Samuel to start dreaming bigger dreams. When we were living out west, he saw a lot of beautiful log homes, and he'd dreamt of building one and then reselling it for a lot of money, but since we didn't have enough money now, it became stressful to live. We all took the brunt of Samuel's wrath. Every day became a struggle, and we all learned to walk carefully on eggshells around his taut mental state.

I tried to encourage my husband and be a good helpmate, as the church told me that I should be, but he told me that it just made him want to kill himself when I talked to him. I wasn't sure what I was doing wrong, but I certainly couldn't get it right. The one thing that I could give him that he enjoyed was my body, so I gave him myself.

I got pregnant and brought another son into the world in February, while we still lived in our makeshift home on one end of the pole barn. With a new midwife and a new herbal tincture that prepared my body for birth, this birth was better than the others, though still being long and painful.

Jacob was a very fussy baby, and Sammy became my best babysitter. When it was cold outside, Sammy pushed baby Jake in circles around the shop on the concrete floor in a stroller. Spring came and warmed up the outdoors enough so that Sammy could push the stroller outside, up and down the driveway. One day, a wheel broke on the stroller. Sammy had literally worn out the wheels of the stroller by pushing Jacob in it so much.

I don't know how I got everything done that year, but I did. During this year, the older kids took on more responsibility. Anna helped me can and freeze all of the food from our large garden. She also milked the family cow each morning and evening at six o'clock sharp. When we had enough cream, she churned it into butter. With the extra milk, we made homemade cheese. Anna may have only been fourteen, but she seemed older than that, and she continued to do more things for me. Since she enjoyed school, she began homeschooling her younger siblings.

As for the older boys, David was responsible for taking care of our two dozen chickens, and Mark went to work with Samuel each day. Samuel decided Mark had enough schooling after sixth grade.

I bought most of the boys' clothes at thrift stores, but I sewed all of the clothes for the girls and me. We worked together to get everything done each day.

Sometimes in the evening, when the kids were playing quietly on the floor, quietly because they got a beating when they weren't quiet, Samuel would suddenly ask them a controversial question. If they disagreed with anything he said, a debate would ensue, and he would get angry, jump up, and get the paddle to beat them. When we were alone, I tried to talk to him about it, but he put me in my place by using Bible verses on how a wife is to obey her husband and keep quiet. And so I learned to be quiet, just like the children.

One morning at the breakfast table, Samuel thought that Mark disrespected him with an expression he made, so he angrily jumped up, grabbed Mark, took him in the bedroom, and beat him.

When the two of them came back out, the rest of us were still just sitting there, as quiet as a group of frightened mice. Samuel could tell that I disapproved of what he had done, even by my nervous silence, so he told me to go outside with him. I followed him, trembling internally.

"What's wrong?" he demanded, his tone and eyes animated with anger.

I fidgeted with my fingers, weighing the decision of whether to be honest with him or not. Daring to choose honesty, I lifted my eyes to meet his. "I think it's wrong to spank the children in anger, Samuel." I dared to defy his authority and his decision by my words, but he had asked for my truth.

He began screaming at me about how I was so disrespectful to his authority and how I was constantly undermining him. He was so full of rage that his eyes nearly popped out of their sockets. I just stood there, shaking as he hurled Bible verses at me.

Feeling ashamed, I regretted my choice to be honest and speak the truth. As he continued on, I thought maybe the way I felt wasn't the truth after all. *Maybe I was wrong.*

Later that day, I went to a little nearby bulk food store to pick up a few necessary things. I numbly roamed the aisles. Midway down the dry goods aisle, I stopped. I looked around and saw nothing but the white walls closing in on me.

What was I supposed to get? I grabbed a bag of beans. Did I need beans? Unsure, I threw it in my empty cart. The bag of beans hit the bottom of the cart with a thud so loud my ears began ringing.

Then I heard the sound of the paddle on my kids' backs. *Whack! Whack!* In a daze, I looked down at the beans and saw a small tear in the bag where I had thrown it in the cart. *My fault.* The torn bag was my fault; the bruises on my kids were my fault. I couldn't even remember what to buy for supper, so clearly, I wasn't a good wife. Samuel just wanted me to be better. I made him angry. It was all my fault that Samuel got angry at the kids and at me. I knew that now. Because of me, nothing ever turned out the way it was supposed to.

After I made my purchase, hoping that I wasn't spending too much money, I got into the van to drive home. Hot tears spilled over as I drove, making it hard for me to see where I was going, when I saw a big semi-truck coming toward me in the opposite lane.

A voice, which I was only familiar with through Samuel's relationship with it, told me to swerve in front of that truck and end my horrible feelings of hopelessness. *Everyone will be better off without you,* it whispered.

It didn't take much to convince me. I was going to do it. I just could not live like this anymore. The truck kept coming nearer, and I knew this was what I was going to do. I had never thought of killing myself before, but I felt trapped and pushed beyond what I could continue to bear.

With tears streaming down my face, I prepared

myself to swerve in front of the semi. I was shaking almost uncontrollably, but I gripped the wheel and tried turning into the other lane. But the wheel would not turn! It just kept me going straight in my lane.

After the semi passed me, a sense of awe washed over me. I could not grasp what had just happened, but deep in my soul, I knew that God did not let me take my life. A sense of love filled my heart, gently nursing the broken pieces of my heart.

In 2003, I got pregnant again. An eighth child. When I was seven months pregnant, Samuel decided to take all of us on a trip fourteen hours south to visit a church in North Carolina.

We were now a family of nine people, and traveling might have been expensive if we didn't know how to do it on a budget. Instead of getting hotel rooms, we slept in the van and stopped at grocery stores along our route to buy white bread and bologna for cheap sandwiches.

Our time in North Carolina was everything that Samuel hoped it would be. On our way home, he told me that he wanted to move there. I silently prayed that we'd have another year in our log home before moving and starting over yet again in a new community.

Two days after we got home and had unpacked all of our suitcases, Samuel was constantly fidgeting, and I knew that either a change or a new storm was on my horizon.

"Anna, we're going to move before the baby is born."

"Why do we have to move so soon?"

"Don't you hear me? I cough so hard every morning that I throw up, the air here in Michigan is too heavy, and I could tell the difference when we were in North Carolina. I felt better, my coughing stopped while we were there."

I had heard Samuel's occasional bouts of coughing, and I worried about him. "Shouldn't you see a doctor about your cough and get some advice? What if there's something you could take for it?"

He shook his head. "If we don't move now, I'm going to die here." He stopped and coughed, but it didn't sound like a real cough.

At my age, in my eighth pregnancy, everything

inside of me revolted against the idea of moving right away. I couldn't accept it. It wouldn't be possible for me to pack the entire house and go through a move before this baby would come. I told him so, and my boldness surprised me. "Samuel, we have to stay in Michigan until after the baby is born. I can't do everything that it takes to move while I'm pregnant."

As I expected, Samuel lit up with rage. "You just can't even handle being pregnant, can you?" He yelled at me before he stormed out of our bedroom.

Even though I expected his anger, it still hurt. I was tired of the way he continuously lashed out at me. I longed for him to ask how I felt or what my opinion was before making a big decision for our family. That night, I silently cried myself to sleep.

Samuel went ahead and began the process of getting ready for our move to North Carolina. A few days later, a Realtor showed up by our front door to look at our house. He was an older guy with a thin layer of hair combed over the top of his balding head. He was bigger than I was at nearly eight months pregnant, and I wondered how he was going to be able to see everything on our large property, but Samuel was in charge. He took Mr. Scott all around our place, the children trailing curiously after the two men.

They were making their way up the basement steps when Mr. Scott stumbled and fell all the way back down the stairs. No one knew that Laura was coming up right behind him, so her body was crushed beneath his weight and then flung along with him as he fell down the stairs. Her screams filled the air, along with the thunderous sounds of Mr. Scott's body hitting the wooden steps.

When Samuel got to her, he carried her limp body upstairs to examine her. She could move her leg, but she couldn't stand on it. I wanted to take her to the hospital immediately, but Samuel didn't see the need.

We took turns and carried Laura around for weeks. She also crawled sideways on the floor to get where she needed to go. It took a couple of months before she could put any weight on that leg, and after a while, she began to walk again.

We moved to North Carolina when baby Ruth was only a couple months old. It had taken several months to find a buyer for our large log home in Michigan.

After we arrived in the south, we lived in a family's two-bedroom basement for several months until Samuel found a new piece of acreage to buy. He found a forty-acre wooded lot in a good location, and then he bought an old, three-bedroom mobile home to put on it for us to live in.

Just like our living arrangement had downsized and deteriorated, our home life continued to deteriorate. Samuel tried starting his own business with no money to even work with, so again, we faced his anger on a daily basis.

We'd only been living in our new community for a few months when Samuel started getting angry with the church leaders for various reasons that fail my memory now. It wasn't long before he was talking about moving west. He would say that he was going to die if we didn't move because he felt sick and he couldn't breathe in the humidity of the south. While I suggested that he go see a doctor for his declining health, he didn't want to let an *Englisha* tell him anything.

Despite his desire to move, we stayed in North

Carolina for four years.

Anna turned seventeen and began going to the outings with the other youth in the church community. After a few outings, she came to me and said, "Dad doesn't treat his family like a father and husband should."

"What do you mean," I asked her, nervously.

She had been in two of her friends' homes and witnessed the love and respect that their fathers displayed toward their wives and children. I felt so troubled over hearing what she was telling me.

She tried to tell me some things about Samuel, but I stopped her. I just couldn't accept it. Fearful of what Samuel would do if he heard her speaking this way, I silenced her. I told her she needed to respect and honor her dad.

A few months went by before Anna came to me one evening, crying. I could tell that she needed to talk to me, but I didn't want Samuel to see us talking or he would want to know what it was about. I'd seen the way he hit her across the face and knocked her out when she was fifteen, simply for looking at him the wrong way.

"Come," I said. "Let's go on a walk." When we were out of sight of the house, I asked her what was wrong.

She was nervous to tell me, afraid that she would get in trouble. "I used a tweezer to pull out the hairs between my eyebrows, Mom. I didn't want to have a unibrow anymore."

I smiled. My daughter was growing up and starting to care about her appearance.

"Dad took me out on the porch this morning and told me that . . ." She switched to a whisper. "He said I'm a whore now, because I plucked around my eyebrows. I just wanted to look nice." Anna burst into tears.

Unsure of how to respond, I tried to comfort her. "You can always come and tell me anything," I offered. I didn't dare discourage her from obeying or respecting her father.

She sniffled. "Dad used to beat us in the shop, and then he said he would hurt us even more if we told you, so I always felt like I couldn't tell you anything."

I was silent. I didn't know what to say. My heart started beating fast at the thought of my small children being beaten when I didn't know about it, despite all the times I did know that they were being beaten.

Anna went on bravely. "When we lived in Kentucky, we helped Dad in the shop. We kept the floors clean, and we were always afraid that a tool would go missing because if it did, even if it wasn't our fault, Dad would beat us, and he would sit us down and tell us how very evil your family is, so I was afraid of being influenced by Aunt Jo when she came to visit us. It was so confusing, and I don't know why that bothers me now, but it just does."

Later, Mark also talked to me about things that happened. I felt devastated and confused. By now, I knew that I could not ignore what they were telling me, but I was at such a loss to know whom to turn to or what to do, and I blamed myself for Samuel's actions.

When I worked up enough courage, I tried talking to the church elders, but all of my fears were confirmed when they encouraged me to be a better and more obedient wife so my husband's anger problem could be taken care of.

Things continued to deteriorate. In desperation, I got books about husband and wife relationships and began reading them. One book taught wives to be a helpmeet and to make their husbands feel like kings. I already did everything that the book outlined as good behavior for a wife, yet Samuel still despised me. But I continued trying.

I began meeting him on the porch with a cold glass of lemonade when he got home from work. I asked him how his day was. Samuel enjoyed my renewed diligence to my wifely duties and confirmed that this was how he wanted to be treated. Yet, he never asked about my day or thanked me for my efforts.

Around this time, I got a set of tapes from one of my sisters who had left the Amish. The series was called The Weigh Down, and it was a weight-loss program. I'll never forget these tapes. They were the beginning of my life changing forever, even though it took years.

The tapes taught me far more than a weight-loss lifestyle. It taught how much God loves us and how perfect we are in his eyes. *Wait. What?* I had to rewind the tape and listen again. That thought was so foreign to me. *God sees me as... perfect?* I could hardly dare to hope it was true. I had my daily devotions religiously and a lot of scriptures were precious to me, but I didn't have a real inner peace that comes from knowing who I was to God.

Well, that all began to change. It felt like scales were slowly crumbling from my eyes. God loved me just the way I was. He cared about every little detail in my life and about me. I carried these new thoughts into my day and thought about them. Slowly, the truth that my spirit already knew began penetrating my heart and mind, transforming me from the inside out.

As I developed this completely new picture of God's love, a love that is never conditional but ever unconditional, I felt like a freed bird with a huge weight lifted from my heart. I had a loving father. I was his loving daughter. I did not have to be good enough, because I was already completely loved just as I was.

Samuel did not understand or like this new person since he wasn't controlling my every thought anymore. I tried to explain how free I felt in God's love, but he didn't understand what I was talking about.

Fired up with rage, he told me that he was going to take a hammer to the tape player.

For the first time, I stood up to him and said, "No, you are not, or I will buy another one."

I hardly recognized the woman that I was becoming, but it felt good to be her. I began voicing some of my thoughts more freely, though I still remained guarded because Samuel was becoming angrier more frequently, and I tried not to provoke his anger.

———————

One day, I heard Samuel yelling at Mark. I didn't know what had happened, but I knew that Samuel's anger toward our son was wrong. I rose up with a calm strength and walked out to place myself between him and Mark.

Samuel's eyes bulged as I stepped between

them, but before he could say anything, I calmly asked, "Is this how a Christian should speak?"

Samuel nearly foamed at the corners of his mouth but said nothing to me.

So I asked him another question: "Are you being a good example to Mark?"

Oh, the look of anger in his eyes was very bad, and in the past, I would have begun shaking, but I just stood there, looking him right in the eyes.

Suddenly, his arm shot up, and his fist was in a tight ball. I got ready for the punch, but it never came. He put his arm back down.

I felt God's protection over me as the warmth of God's love spread completely through me.

8.

THE ACCIDENT

Summer 2007

We moved to Potlatch, Idaho, the middle of nowhere. On our way out west, we dropped off a few things for Anna in Colorado. Anna had gotten married soon after she turned nineteen, but life threw her a couple of curveballs soon afterward. As a result, she and her new husband moved to Colorado after getting excommunicated from the Mennonite church in North Carolina.

Potlatch, Idaho, was rough since we didn't know anyone, and we had no plain community to be part of. We couldn't even attend church as there were no plain churches nearby.

While I had my newfound faith in God, everyday life was hard for our family. We moved into a small house, with very little to live on because Samuel didn't have much work. It was much harder to grow a garden in northern Idaho because the nights would get very cold and the seasons were short. Samuel and the boys started building storage sheds to sell, while I homeschooled the youngest children.

Anna's husband decided to join the military, so in the middle of a fiercely cold winter, she asked Samuel if she could stay with us while he was in boot camp. Samuel agreed. I was so happy because I missed her so much since she had gotten married.

Anna helped me with the homeschooling and housework, just like she had when she still lived at home. One Saturday evening, she gave all the boys haircuts, which was a skill that she'd taught herself over the years. She had been the trusted family barber for the boys and Samuel.

I listened to the siblings talking with each other. She, Mark, and David were talking about finding a church to attend the next day. I smiled, joy filling my heart to know that my children wanted to go to church. They wouldn't be able to find a plain church, but that no longer mattered to me. I knew that God wasn't found in the religious culture of my upbringing—God was God; God was everywhere.

After they left the next morning, Samuel was in a bad mood, and it wasn't long before he pulled me into the bedroom. "I'm going to have to ask Anna to leave."

This wasn't what I expected him to say. "Why?"

"She just came here, and she's trying to take over my home!" He fumed. "Just look at the boys' haircuts! They don't even look plain!" His voice grew louder, and his words came out faster, on and on. He was angry that they had gone to church, and not a plain church at that.

I couldn't understand what was wrong with them going to church, and as for the haircuts, I thought they looked fine. They were shorter than the way we usually cut their hair, but I just couldn't see how that mattered. Everything that Samuel was angry about seemed too trivial to me.

"Samuel," I interjected, "isn't it a good thing that our children want to seek God and go to church?"

"You know it's not right! It's not a plain church. There aren't any Anabaptist types of churches around here for them to go to, so no, it's not good."

He simply couldn't see the irony of the situation. For months, we had been sitting at home every Sunday with no devotions or any spiritual food to speak of, and now he was angry that his children had gone to church.

As soon as the three oldest children got home, Samuel stormed out of the house and started talking to them. I followed him.

"Anna, you're going to have to leave."

I watched the look of shock that filled her eyes.

"Why, Dad?"

"You know why."

"But, I really don't. I don't know why." Her voice was soft, pleading with her father.

"You come up in here, into my house, and you're trying to take over my home. You know what you're doing; I know you do." He spat into the ground.

"Dad," her voice trembled, "what did I do to make you think that?"

Before he could answer, Mark spoke up. "Dad, if you're going to kick Anna out, then I'm going to leave with her."

"Okay, go ahead! Leave!"

"Samuel, please don't do this." I begged, but he wouldn't listen. He started railing on Anna, screaming at her about everything she'd done wrong since stepping foot inside the house.

I watched her face change from shock to strength as she stood still and met her dad's rage with a calmness that I recognized. She wasn't afraid of her father anymore.

All of sudden, Samuel turned and started hitting the truck with his fists. Mark grabbed his dad and wrestled him to the ground, pinning him down to the ground till he calmed down. Samuel may have calmed down, but he was still angry. Mark and Anna decided to leave, just like he'd asked them to do.

Mark called their cousin, who lived several hours away, and he said they could stay with him and his wife. I was so scared for my two oldest. I wished I at least had some money to give them, but I had nothing. Samuel never let me have any cash.

I was the most worried about Anna. She was fifteen weeks pregnant, and she had already had two miscarriages. With all the stress she was under with being away from her husband, then being totally rejected by her dad, it could be too much for her body to handle.

After Anna and Mark left with their cousin, I told Samuel that I had absolutely no respect for him anymore.

Two weeks later, I got a call from Mark. He told me that he'd found Anna in the bathroom during the night after hearing her cry out. She was bleeding out on the bathroom floor, so they called 911, and she was taken to the hospital in an ambulance. When she woke up, she started asking for me.

It was the worst kind of news that I could hear, and I was so scared for my daughter. I asked Samuel if he could take me to her. He said no. Since I had no way of going on my own, I told Mark I was sorry, but I couldn't come.

I didn't know what to do except to pray fervently for Anna and for Mark. Right after my prayer, the phone rang, and it was Samuel's mom. He talked with her for just a few minutes. When he got off the phone, he told me to get ready and pack a bag. He'd changed his mind. He was going to take me to be with Anna. Mark had called his Grosmommy because he knew that his dad would listen to her. I was so proud of my son's persistence and his care for his sister.

Anna lost both of her babies. She had been pregnant with twins. Mark and I just held her, crying and praying with her. It was nearly more than I could bear to watch her suffer like that. I felt so helpless. Why did this have to happen? I prayed that God would heal my daughter's heart and body.

When Anna's husband was finished with boot camp, they moved to their new station at a military base in Missouri. Mark moved in with a friend in Colorado. He was able to work with his friend in his diesel shop, and he loved this type of work. While being away was best for them, I missed both of my children.

———————

I disobeyed Samuel when the children and I began attending a local, non-plain church. Perhaps that's why he believed that I was punished for my sin, when the accident happened that fateful morning in July.

One moment I was on my way to church; the next moment, I came face to face with eternity. A large truck was hurtling toward us in our lane. Impact was inevitable.

It was a Sunday morning, like any other morning. Life was simple as we dressed for church. With our small car, the children had been taking turns going to church with me. Our church's worship service began an hour early in the summer season so that left us with a little less time to get ready. Usually, we didn't take the time to grab breakfast before heading out the door and this morning was no exception.

David (17), Sammy (14), Laura (9), and I climbed into our silver Mazda car. All of our seatbelt buckles clicked. Everyone wore their seat belts without a second thought, out of habit. It was precisely 8:30 a.m. as we pulled out of our driveway.

David was driving. Sammy sat opposite of him in the passenger seat. Laura and I shared the back seat. I was sitting directly behind Sammy. We decided to take a road less traveled, a road open only to local traffic because of road construction. Since our property bordered this highway, we had legal access.

Our conversation turned to our plans for the day. After church, we were going to buy a kite for the younger kids and stop at WinCo to buy a few groceries. A few miles down the road, David turned on some music. As we rode along, watching the beautiful rolling wheat land slip by us, we listened to the words of "Bad Day" by Daniel Powter. We rounded a curve in the road to see a large truck coming toward us in our lane.

David slammed on his brakes. As tires screeched, our car kept sliding toward the oncoming vehicle. He whipped slightly into the other lane just before the crash to try and avoid colliding with our larger counterpart.

In the instant before impact, he said, "Oh, this isn't going to be too bad." Moments later, in a halt between his siblings' screams, he said, "This is a dream. We're all going to wake up soon. This has to be a dream."

At the moment of collision, my breath was knocked out of me. My ears were filled with the piercing sound of metal against metal, knife-like, a horrible crunching as the car twisted and my body was slammed forward. In the intense sensation of shock, everything went into slow motion. I saw a flash of white and then black in front of my eyes. A horrible taste permeated me; I felt it was the taste of death.

All of the children began screaming as I tried to breathe. I couldn't scream. I couldn't move. I was paralyzed in the position where I was pinned to the seat, underneath the smashed roof of the car.

My mouth had gone dry, still filled with that horrible taste. I tried to open my mouth to talk to the children, and a very weak voice came out that was not my own.

In the moment of our tragedy, pain was much larger than life, the situation seemed so surreal. All I could think was to try and comfort my children. Laura's and my back screamed with pain. I still couldn't move.

My children kept crying out and yelling that this was all a dream. Sammy kept slipping in and out of consciousness. In our pain, I realized we were all alive. We were *alive*.

When I found my voice, I said, "No, this isn't a dream, but everything is going to be okay."

The man in the truck got out of his vehicle, unharmed. He quickly called 911. Somehow David found my cell phone on the floor and handed it to me so I could call Samuel, and he came to the scene of the accident. The man from the truck gave us a bottle of water.

After what seemed like an eternity, paramedics arrived. Since the main impact was on Sammy's and my side of the car, David and Laura got out first.

Then Sammy and I were covered with towels as they began to cut off the roof of the vehicle to get us out. One of the medics spoke gently to me.

He explained why they needed to put towels over us and kept asking me what my name was and what day it was. All I could think about was my pain.

He watched so that nothing fell down on me and tried to make me as comfortable as possible. Another medic and Samuel kept talking to Sammy to keep him conscious.

Once it was safe to do so, I was removed so they could pull Sammy's seat back and get him out. His left wrist was twisted and bent at a strange angle. His upper right leg was also bent.

Laura and I were put into an ambulance before Sammy was removed from the car. All of the paramedics were so caring, but as we drove away, I kept worrying about him.

Laura and I arrived at the hospital in Pullman, WA, across the state line, while David and Sammy were taken to a hospital in Moscow, ID. Laura was taken care of first when we arrived. They took X-rays and a CAT scan to find out if she had any broken bones.

After a thorough examination, they released her with only a few bruises. How thankful I was that no bones were broken in my daughter's body!

After examining me, a gray-haired doctor pulled back the long white curtain to tell me that because my back injuries were extensive, I would be airlifted to a spinal trauma center in Seattle, WA. He told me that someone with more experience would need to explain what my specific injuries were. He showed me the X-rays of my back and pointed out that I had several crushed and cracked vertebrae, and that several of my ribs were broken.

I also learned that my liver had been bruised in the accident, and they were going to keep a careful watch on my condition. Most of my injuries were caused by the impact of being pulled back by my seatbelt, but without my seatbelt, I would likely have been killed. I still had a horrible taste in my mouth and asked for a drink of water. One of the nurses gave me a few sips.

Debbie and Jackie, who we hardly knew from the church, came to see us. I had only met Jackie a few weeks ago at a church picnic. Yet, both of these beautiful ladies lifted their hands over me and began to pray.

I was overwhelmed that God answered my prayer before I even had time to ask it. Another family took Laura home with them until Samuel could go and pick her up.

David's collar bone was broken. Fourteen stitches went into the deep gash on his ankle. Again, his injuries were fairly minor.

Then I got a call that Sammy was being transferred to a larger hospital over an hour away for surgery on both his leg and wrist. The femur bone in his right leg was broken. His wrist was also in bad shape.

Samuel was trying to figure out how to divide his time between all three hospitals. After David had been released, they went to pick up Laura, and then they drove the distance to the hospital where Sammy was being transferred. Samuel needed to sign a paper to release Sammy for his surgery.

Finally, they came to the hospital where I was. Since I was floating in and out of consciousness and strapped into braces, I didn't know they were there until I saw Samuel's face above me.

At the scene of the accident, he'd worked calmly and patiently with Sammy, assuring all of us that everything would be alright. I felt grateful that he was so kind to us, and I searched his face now for the same kindness.

Instead, his eyes had turned black with hatred and disgust. "You always cost me money, don't you?" he said. All Samuel could think about was the money that our hospital bills would cost him.

Before I drifted back into unconsciousness, I vowed to myself that I would find a way to leave him.

An AirLift crew came into my room and took over preparing me for my transfer to Harborview Medical Center. One of the members bent over me and exclaimed that I needed a more comfortable neck brace. All of them were professional yet caring. This was comforting as my body was in their hands. They had to move me, but moving was so painful.

Before I knew it, I was in a small airplane. The crew surrounded me, checking my blood pressure and adjusting my neck brace. My mind felt hazy as we flew smoothly through the air. When we arrived at Harborview, nurses began to prepare me for more X-rays and another CAT scan.

It was a long night. I was in a constant blur of pain. My mouth was dry and tasted horrible. I wasn't hungry, I just wanted a drink. I asked for water, but I wasn't allowed to have any because I was scheduled for surgery within the next twenty-four hours. Oh, how I longed for a bit of sweet, cool water on my tongue.

Finally, a kind girl came into my room with a chip of ice swimming on a plastic spoon. "Here," she whispered, "this is just between you and me." My angel visited my room several more times throughout the night with small chips of ice to cool my tongue.

The next day, Monday, slipped in without me noticing. I couldn't think much about anything. Information about what was wrong with my body and my predicted recovery of many months with a body cast and finally body braces swam in front of me. Then because of my bruised liver, my surgery was delayed. I was passing blood, and my blood count was dropping.

I received a few more phone calls from my family. Anna cried bravely into the phone, thankful that I was alive. She had been so worried about me, like everyone else. Her husband was already buying a one-way plane ticket for her to come and help take care of all of us for as long as we needed her.

An even longer thirty hours after my arrival at Harborview, I was wheeled into the operating room. Both of the anesthetists talked to me as they put me to sleep. As my vision grew blurry, I heard them saying that my chance of being blind after this operation was one in a thousand. Before I had a chance to think about my two choices in life, either to be blind or to be paralyzed, I was out. My surgery lasted a total of five hours, and I was given six blood transfusions to replace the amount of blood I lost in surgery.

Later, in the recovery room, I opened my eyes. The lights seemed so far away. Why are the lights so dim in this room? I wondered as I drifted in and out of consciousness. I thought I remembered waking up in the middle of my surgery screaming that I was in so much pain, that I couldn't take the pain anymore. *Was I dreaming? Was I imagining things?* Details were a blur; nothing made sense.

After a while, a nurse came in to tell me that my surgery had been successful and I wouldn't need a body cast or brace. Relief flooded me as I understood what she was telling me.

The following day I had a visitor. My new-found friend Debbie called a Pastor whom she was friends with in Seattle, and he came in to pray with me. An aunt of a friend of mine also came to see me. She felt bad disturbing me because I could hardly talk, and my eyes kept drooping.

The rest of the day passed by as I slept.

In the evening, they brought me my first meal. Small swirls of steam rose above the foam container of chicken broth. The last time I ate or drank anything had been three days earlier.

Weakly, I sipped a small amount of the broth, and it burned my tongue. I tried to set it down. The container slipped from my hands, spilling all over my tray and down on my blanket. I was so embarrassed.

A nurse came in to clean up the mess that I made, and then everything was carried away. My stomach felt like a flat, empty puddle. I closed my eyes and focused on my breathing. Soon I fell asleep again.

The next morning, I'd lost track of which day it was, my serving tray held small cartons of milk and juice, a bit of cereal in a small container, and quiche. I sampled a bit of everything. Instead of feeling strength from what I was able to nibble on, I felt lightheaded and dizzy as my heart raced.

Soon nurses came into my room to get me up out of bed for the first time. It took a lot of joint effort. We went slowly. I could only breathe very shallowly because of my broken ribs. Focusing on each movement in part, I realized everything I'd ever taken for granted was now a feat to accomplish.

In the evening, a young man poked his head through the door. "Are you Anna Troyer?" He said he was from a church group that had heard about the accident and my situation. His name was Chris. His wife had been feeling sick, so she wasn't able to come with him. He prayed for me. How encouraged I felt. It seemed that real angels in the form of caring people kept coming into my room to bless me and pray over me.

A nurse said it was Thursday now. Five days since the accident. Five days since I had seen my family. Again I got up and walked with the help of my nurses. Again I was surprised by a visit from the same pastor who came to pray with me earlier in the week. This kind, gray-haired man held my hands as he prayed to God to heal me. His son was getting married on Saturday, yet he took the time to walk down the hallways of this big hospital to come to my room, sit down to talk to me and pray for me. He was another human angel.

A day later, the doctor approved my release, and Samuel made quick plans to come to Seattle to pick me up. He rented a van and put a mattress in the back of it. Soon he and Mose were on their way.

They reached Harbor View around four o'clock in the afternoon. Before we could leave, we had to pick up my prescriptions from the pharmacy in the hospital. Then they wheeled me to where the van was waiting. They got me into the back of the van onto the mattress and tried to make me comfortable.

The eight-hour trip home from Seattle turned into a twelve-hour nightmare. I felt every bump in the road. Each bump took my breath away with pain and fear that the bumping was going to hurt my back all over again. Very soon, I was out of breath, and my ribs racked with pain.

When I cried out, Samuel stopped the van to give me a break from the bumping and swaying motion. He tried to adjust me to a more comfortable position, but it seemed to be of no use. The bumping went on forever as we crept along. In the early morning hours of the night, we eased over the bumps up the steep driveway up to our house.

Home. I was finally *home*.

The next morning, I took in the sweet smiles of my children. They were eager to show me the "Welcome Home" banner that they made for me. As they bravely surrounded me with their angelic faces, I knew that my pain was worth it to still be here with them, though I wished they didn't have to see me so white and frail.

I didn't know what lay ahead of me in my recovery. But maybe the pain was there to open my eyes to the angels all around me, human angels of mercy. They came around me, picking me up between them, lending their wings with hearts of servants to lift me closer to God and closer to complete healing.

I was so thankful to have Anna there to help all of us. This time, Samuel didn't accuse her of trying to take over his house. We all needed her. I needed help getting up and using the bathroom. She cleaned my surgery cuts, changed my bandages every day, and helped Sammy, who couldn't move on his own with a broken femur in his thigh and a shattered wrist. There was so much to do, yet she never complained.

A few days after I got home, the family that had taken care of Laura when she was released from the hospital called me and asked if they could take her with them to help with their horses. Laura had told them she loved horses.

I was so blessed that they were reaching out and thought it would be so good for Laura, especially with all the trauma she had just gone through. Well, Samuel did not approve. He said she couldn't go. I begged him to let her go, letting him know it would surely be good for her.

A black, evil darkness darkened his eyes as he leaned over me while I lay helplessly beneath him in bed.

"You are so evil and that is why you were in this accident." He cursed me, "God is punishing you, and I am going to divorce you."

I could feel all of his demons staring at me, but suddenly, I felt a strength rising up deep within my soul. I just stared right back at those demons, not saying one word. But I heard a quiet whisper in my heart: *you will leave him as soon as you get strong enough.*

I was once again in awe as I felt God's love protecting me and reassuring me that he would take care of the children and me.

One day Anna and David were whispering and acting strange. Then Anna told me that she needed to run to town. David was still acting suspicious, but I kind of just let it go. He kept smiling, then checking out the window after a while.

Then the front door opened and in walked my oldest son, Mark! It was just so good to see him! And finally, once again, I had all my beautiful kids surrounding me. There was no better gift that my children could give me than their presence.

It was a long summer, fall, and winter as we slowly regained our strength. Anna stayed and helped us for six weeks. I was so sad when she left again.

9.

THE GETAWAY

Spring 2009

After the accident, Samuel got a TV for our house. That was completely unexpected, and it was nice, since we had to sit so much and had nothing to do as the weeks of our recovery drug slowly by. It was fun to be able to watch some TV. Old black-and-white TV shows were my favorite shows to watch.

One day Laura was watching a kids show when Samuel came in for a break from work and wanted to tune into the news. Instead of telling Laura that he wanted to watch the news, he ripped the remote out of her hands and changed the channel.

Of course, that disappointed her, but she didn't dare talk back to her father, so she simply left the room and started going upstairs to her room.

Samuel didn't like the attitude change that he sensed in her, so he jumped off the couch and started yelling at her. He ran up the stairs, grabbed her by her ankles, and jerked her down the stairs before taking her into our bedroom. I started shaking the moment he jumped up from the couch because I could sense his rage, and I knew that something bad was going to happen.

The rest of the children and I stood around and watched what was happening to Laura, as if we were watching a movie. All at once, I snapped out of my daze and went to the bedroom where Samuel had begun beating our young daughter.

I heard myself yelling at him. "Stop! You are not going to hit her in anger!"

He raised his arm, and again I got ready for him to start hitting me. His look of dark rage made the hair stand up on the back of my neck, but I did not back down.

Suddenly, he just put his arm down and walked out. I went to Laura and hugged her. We were both shaking and crying.

In March, David told me that he wanted to go live with Anna and her husband in Missouri. Samuel said that it was okay. I was so sad. One day I asked him why he wanted to leave. He told me with tears in his eyes that he didn't want to stay with his dad and be treated the way Mark had been. I was heartbroken, but I gave him my blessing to leave us.

I had been praying that God would help me and the children get away from Samuel. My three oldest children said they would do anything they could to help us leave. Mark told me that he was very worried since his dad's behavior had been getting worse with anger and depression.

Samuel had told him he was going to shoot all of us and then shoot himself. Afraid he was going to carry out the threat, Mark said it was time for me to leave as soon as possible.

One night as we were going to bed, Samuel came over and grabbed me. "I just want to rape you right now." I knew he wanted to hurt me and that scared me. At the time, I didn't realize that he had often raped me over the years. All of those times after having a baby, when he forced himself on me without my consent, was rape. Even in marriage, sex has to be consensual. But at the time, I didn't see it that way.

Our daughter Anna was pregnant again and due in November. I was so excited to finally become a grandma. She and I talked a lot on the phone. She had shared my situation with her bible study group, and she told me that the ladies were all praying for me. One of the ladies in Anna's group offered to have us stay in her house for a few months. I was overwhelmed by God's goodness. Now, I just had to find a way to leave Samuel with all the kids.

One morning God gave me a special verse from Proverbs 16:3: Commit your actions to the Lord, and your plans will succeed. I knew it was my promise, and I claimed it. I knew God was making a way, and I just continued to pray for our safety.

Once our plan was in place, Anna called Samuel. She asked him if the kids and I could come stay with her for a month after her baby was born. She reminded him that she had helped us out after the accident, and she really wanted me there to help with the baby.

I know that God made Samuel say yes because

he would never have agreed to let us go. I was so excited yet afraid. Only Anna, Mark, and David knew what was happening.

I really didn't know how to pack. I told the kids to take their favorite stuffed animals and blankets. I looked around my home and wondered what I would miss? But the only things that mattered to me and that I could not do without were my kids. It seemed so unreal that I would not be back. I was finally getting away from this nightmare of a life.

Feeling afraid of the unknown, I worried about how I would support five kids. I had been a stay-at-home mom my entire life. I never had a job, besides cleaning houses with my sisters when I was younger. There were so many questions that I could not answer, but they did not make me question for one second if I was doing the right thing. I knew my God was making a way for the kids and me to have a better life, and that was all that mattered.

It was a long, cold drive from Idaho to Missouri. I tried not to act nervous, since I didn't want Samuel to suspect anything. Little did he know that he was taking us to a new life, mile after mile. The children and I were so excited to meet Anna's new baby. We had seen lots of pictures, and she was so beautiful. Laura had embroidered a pillow for her, and I had sewn a crib-sized quilt for her. I could hardly wait to hold my granddaughter in my arms.

Finally, we arrived in Missouri. Anna's husband met us at the visitor center to sign us onto the military base. Samuel stayed a few days to help Anna and her little family move to a new house. He hugged everyone goodbye and headed home to run his barn business, thinking that he would be back in a month to bring us home.

After Samuel left, we moved over to Anna's friend's house. In the mornings we did our homeschooling, then after lunch we went over to help Anna and her baby. One day when I went over to Anna's house to call Samuel, she offered to sit with me while I called him.

She told me that, no matter what happened, whatever Samuel did after I called him was not my responsibility. She knew that he was always threatening to kill himself, and she told me that if he chose to end his own life that I was not responsible, but it was his choice.

I was so grateful for my daughter's advice. It

was still intimidating, but I knew that I was finally free from any condemnation from Samuel! I had lived with that fear for over twenty-five years! I felt so blessed as Anna held my hands and prayed with me before I made the call.

Shaking, I dialed his cell number. He picked up, and we chatted a few minutes. I told him I was glad he made it home safely.

Then I said, "Samuel, I have something to tell you." For a moment, I thought about every decision he'd made and told me about. Decisions that I couldn't make for myself. This time, I was making my own decision. Nervously, I told him what I had tried to prepare myself to say.

"The kids and I are not coming back home. I have pleaded with you that things need to change, and you have refused to listen." And then, because I felt like I needed to offer him a road back to me, I continued, "I would really like it if you made an appointment with a medical doctor and got on some medication for your anxiety and health problems. I would also like it if you could start seeing a therapist to overcome your anger."

He was so angry. He said he would come and

get us and bring us back home. But I felt so safe because we were on a military base, and no one could get on the base unless a family member agreed to let them in. For the first time since I had married Samuel, I felt completely safe. I was finally free. I just praised and thanked our God for being so good to us.

Even though I knew I was not responsible if he decided to kill himself, I still worried. Later he confirmed that he did try, but then didn't go through with it.

Samuel actually did go to see a doctor. He gave the doctor my number, so after his visit, the doctor called me with a diagnosis. In just one visit, she could tell Samuel has extreme anxiety and anger problems. She gave him a prescription for anxiety and told him he needed to go to anger management.

He told me he took only a few of the pills and quit, because he almost died from them. He claimed he woke up one night and could not breathe, then started throwing up. I told him to go back to the doctor and tell her, and she could have him try a different medication. He refused. However, he agreed to go see the pastor at the church we attended to start some counseling with him.

I had not yet realized that even though I had physically left Samuel, I was still mentally caught in his endless web of empty promises, clinging to hope that he would change.

10.

THE WEB

Spring 2010

The children and I were finally free to be loud and play games together. At first, our freedom felt strange because we weren't used to it. We hardly knew what to do with ourselves. What fun it was to be free!

I turned the radio up to listen to a local Christian station, which I could never listen to freely before. The children could laugh and run around without being yelled at, and we could have family discussions without the fear of getting scolded or beaten.

Our lives were changing so much, so I sat down with each child individually and explained to them that we were not going back home. I felt guilty when they were sad over leaving some of their things at home, but, at least, they had a few of their things.

We lived in Missouri for two months while I prayed every day for God to lead me. I thought about renting a place there, but when Anna and I talked about that option, we realized that she and her husband could be called to another military base at any time, and I really wanted to be near family.

Samuel had called Anna to tell her that he was coming to Missouri to visit his parents, who had moved about two hours from where we were living. He asked if he could see the children. I didn't feel safe and was frightened to see him again, but Anna assured me it would be okay, and we could leave at any time if things were not going well. She made the arrangements for us to meet him at a restaurant in a nearby town.

I had been in contact with Samuel through email, and he told me that he was attending church since I left and had gone through a spiritual deliverance and was a changed man. I wanted so much to believe him. I was very skeptical, but I wanted to give him another chance.

When we met Samuel for dinner, I was surprised to see him smiling and happy. I could hardly believe it, since he had so seldomly smiled. I thought he was going to be angry with me and threaten me, but he was calm and pleasant. Did I dare to hope that he had really changed? I wanted to. I wanted to believe he could be different.

Samuel spoke so kindly to us, but after just a little bit, he completely ignored the kids and only talked to me. I did not like that, but I was glad to see him actually happy, so I didn't want to be too critical of his behavior. It was so strange and different to see him like this. Did I dare to hope that he and I could get back together and actually have a happy marriage?

All of my questions swirled through my mind, making me feel nauseous. Even though Samuel seemed happy, something didn't feel right, and the stress of it all made me feel suffocated. I had just started my period and my flow had been quite heavy. Suddenly I felt really tired and wanted to leave.

By the time we got back to Anna's house, I was nearly hemorrhaging, and it scared me. I picked up the phone and called my midwife, still mentally trained not to call a medical doctor. My midwife told me that I was probably bleeding so much because I had been under so much stress. She told me to lie down, put several pillows under my legs, and hold completely still. It still took a few hours, but my heavy bleeding finally slowed down.

I finally decided to move to Michigan, close to my sister Josephine and her family. Some of our kids were close to the same age, and I could put the kids into public school so I could get a job to support us. Mark drove in from Colorado to help. He and David helped me rent a little Uhaul trailer to pull behind the van and we all drove to Michigan.

I enrolled the kids in public school for the first time in their lives. Everything about this life was new for all of us. When I left Samuel, I left my plain way of thinking and embraced the changes of a more mainstream lifestyle.

I took the girls shopping at Goodwill, where they picked out jeans and T-shirts to wear. Laura wanted to get her ears pierced, so we went to the mall and had our ears pierced together. That was a bit painful, and it felt strange to look in the mirror each day to see those tiny glittering studs in my ears.

When we were living in Missouri, Anna had a friend who was a hairstylist, and she gave me a short haircut. I loved how easy it was to take care of my new hair.

I found an apartment to rent, and life seemed to be settling into a normal routine. After our accident, I received a settlement that was large enough for us to live on for a while. But since I still had a lot of pain in my back, I wasn't able to work yet.

Samuel called soon after his visit, and I picked up because we'd started talking again.

"Hey, Anna," he greeted me in a bright tone of voice. His nice behavior had continued since our meetup in Missouri, and I looked forward to his calls with hope in my heart that better days were ahead of us.

We chatted about the weather and the children. I didn't tell him certain things for fear of triggering his rage, a fear that had been ingrained in me for more than twenty-five years. It was better to keep him happy. After all, I enjoyed a happy Samuel.

"You deserve to be treated better, Anna." His

quick switch in topic caught me off guard. "I mean it. I'm sorry for treating you the way I did."

I blinked at the instant tears that sprang to my eyes, pressing the phone against my ear. Had I heard Samuel correctly? Was he really apologizing to me? Did he really mean it? What did this mean? Could we be a family again? I wasn't sure how to respond, and I suddenly felt nervous, fearful of saying the wrong thing. I listened to him as he kept talking.

"Anna, I understand if you say no, but I really want to come for a visit. Can I come?" He sounded like a young, eager boy on the other side of the line, and I heard myself saying yes.

———————

Samuel came for a weekend in May, bringing papers for me to sign. He surprised me by selling our place in Idaho. I knew how much Samuel loved living out west, and every time I imagined the possibility of our family being back together again, I pictured us moving back to Idaho. I had really enjoyed our church there, but then again, maybe it was better if we started over in Michigan, near my family.

Samuel took me out on a real date. He shaved and dressed nicely for the evening. Relaxed, he smiled into my eyes and told me how beautiful I looked. We went to a restaurant for dinner before going to the movie theater and watching the romantic comedy, *Date Night.* Samuel and I had never gone to see a movie before. I could hardly believe the beautiful evening that we were sharing together. It felt too good to be true.

After the movie was over, we kissed. It felt familiar and new all at the same time. Samuel told me how much he missed me and the kids. He wiped a tear away when he expressed to me how hard it had been to be all alone, without the children and me there. Now he knew that our family was worth fighting for, and he wanted to go to counseling and work on reconciliation with me.

Hope swirled around my heart at the sound of his words, supported by the kindness that Samuel was showing me. This was not like the Samuel I knew at all. He was kind, doting, unusually easy going, and positive about life. Who was this man? Suddenly I felt suffocated and confused by everything that I needed to figure out but that didn't make sense because, after all, Samuel had changed.

I asked this new version of Samuel if we could go to marriage counseling with the pastor of the church I had been attending with my sister. He agreed. Again, I was pleasantly surprised. So even though the pastor was very busy and we made the request for counseling on a very short notice, he made time to see us.

Pastor Nate patiently listened to some of our history, focusing his questions on what led to our marital separation. Thoughtful, he leaned back as I talked. When it came time to open up about the abuse, I worried this part of the session would make Samuel angry. I tried to protect him as much as I could, giving him whatever credit I could for all of the changes I'd seen in him at our meetup, our handful of phone calls, and this unusually happy weekend that we'd just spent together.

"Hmmm." Pastor Nate finally seemed ready to say something. First, he turned to Samuel. "Do you understand why your wife needed to leave?"

Samuel nodded. I was surprised and relieved to see him willingly acknowledging that he understood my pain.

"She is like a fierce mama bear, with the instinct to protect her cubs. She had to leave you when you weren't making any effort to change your family's situation or your behavior." He paused.

I felt Samuel stiffen beside me, and my palms felt clammy. I still feared Samuel's rage. I hadn't known a version of him that wasn't prone to sullen mood swings and hot flashes of anger. I felt relieved when the pastor's attention shifted back to both of us.

Pastor Nate told us it would be a lot of hard work but not impossible to restore our marriage. He challenged us both to be willing to give our all to the relationship.

I was willing and ready to start. Samuel agreed. He was ready, too.

Then, the pastor gave me a number of a Christian counselor because he felt that I needed to talk to someone about the abuse I had suffered. He also gave us a number to a family counselor and a list of a few books that he said would be helpful to read together. At the end, we made another appointment to go back to see him.

Samuel's weekend visit had just become permanent.

We bought a small place close to town. Samuel put in some new floors and fixed a few other issues with the house. He wanted to start building storage sheds again, but he had sold most of his tools, leaving the rest of it in Missouri at his folks' place.

I suggested that since he was always so stressed with trying to run a business, it might be less stressful if he just got a job somewhere, at least while we were trying to repair our marriage. Samuel didn't like that idea, but he didn't get angry with me, and I was glad for that.

While things with Samuel were looking good, my health issues were flaring up again. I was struggling to find the energy I needed to make it through the day without a nap. I found a large lump in my side which really scared me, but when I went to see a gynecologist, she said it was only some fatty tissue. She told me that she could remove it at her office to save me money since I did not have insurance.

I was still experiencing very heavy bleeding each month, so my gynecologist suggested an endometrial ablation. She said it would most likely stop any monthly periods after a few months. That sounded like an amazing solution.

First, I went in for the endometrial ablation procedure. Then I was scheduled to come back for the removal of the fatty tumor on my side. When the gynecologist opened me up, it was bigger than she had anticipated, and it ended up being a very painful process for her to remove all of it, even though she kept trying to keep the area numb.

That night I was in a lot of pain, so I went to bed early. A while later Samuel came to bed. He wanted to have sex. I could hardly believe it. I was exhausted, and I needed to recover from the procedure that I went through mere hours ago.

Samuel said that in his counseling in Idaho, he was told that having a lot of sex was the best way to heal a marriage. I still don't believe this is how they explained it to him, but this was what he heard, and he wanted to practice his right to have sex with me while I was still in pain. Perhaps my inability to fight back and my physical vulnerability turned him on.

I didn't wait for Samuel to force himself on me. I just made up an excuse and left the room. I went downstairs and slept on the recliner that night. It was then I realized he had not really changed but was only pretending so I would take him back.

That old, familiar feeling had crept back into my body. I was afraid again. I was trapped in a web that I could not seem to get out of. It would only be a matter of time before Samuel would physically hurt me again.

Samuel refused to go to our next counseling session with Pastor Nate. He felt like the pastor just picked on him and put all the blame on him. He sat around the house that day, like he'd been doing every day. He didn't try to look for work, and I hardly knew what to do with him. I should not have been so eager to get back together. My bliss was gone and life was starting to go back to exactly as it had always been.

One Sunday morning before going to church, I was watching a sermon by Joyce Meyers. I can't remember what the sermon was about, but suddenly, Samuel jumped up and looked at me with animated rage all over his stature. "I just want to choke you!" he screamed at me. Then he stormed outside.

I got up and got the children ready to go to church with an unsettled feeling in the pit of my stomach. The storm had come back, and we all felt it.

Samuel didn't go to church with us, and later he went over to my sister's house. He told her and her husband that he wanted to kill me. Scared he would follow through, they tried to calm him down and asked him if we could both come over that evening to talk. He agreed.

I hoped that my sister and her husband would be able to help us. It seemed like everything was crumbling around me, and a heavy fog was seeping into my mind.

Josephine and her husband shared that they had also gone to marriage counseling at different times. They told us it can take months or even years to repair a marriage. Samuel didn't agree. He couldn't take that much time and felt just going to one counseling session should have been enough. As the conversation went on, he deflected and pointed out all my weaknesses. It was a long, hard evening that left me feeling even more confused.

When Jo or her husband would ask Samuel a

question, he would give an evasive answer. We were not making any progress. It was just a vicious cycle of him throwing accusations at me. Finally, Jo's husband advised Samuel to go somewhere for a while. Get a job and try to figure things out. He mentioned that there was a lot of cleanup work in Florida from the recent hurricane.

The next day after our long evening at my sister's house, Samuel told me that he was going to go out to Colorado and pick up the skid steer machine he had given Mark, then head to Florida to find work.

"Wait, you're going to take the skid steer away from Mark? You told him you were sorry for never paying him when he worked for you so you gave that machine to him. What are you going to tell him now?"

"Well, that machine cost me a lot of money, and I am going to get it back," Samuel said.

I told him that I could not agree to do this to our son. I asked him to call Pastor Nate and make an appointment so we could ask his advice. Samuel said that it was none of Pastor Nate's business what he did. I tried to continue reasoning with him, but it was pointless.

Once again, Samuel was going to break a promise he made to Mark. I felt sick over it. So many times I had worried about my kids, especially my sons. I wondered how they could have any faith in God after all the beatings and emotional abuse that they lived through. To make it even worse, Samuel used the Bible to condemn all of us.

I remembered the time when Mark told me, "Mom, if it weren't for your Christian example, I would not even believe in God." I held my son and cried. It made me feel good to know that I inspired his faith in God, and yet at the same time, I felt so sad that he did not have a godly example in his earthly father.

Samuel's mind was made up again. He was going to Colorado to steal back the machinery that he'd given his son as payment for more than ten years of free labor.

As Samuel was leaving, I asked him to send money home from Florida to help support the children. He told me he would rot in jail before he paid me one cent, and then he left.

I called Mark. I wanted to warn him that his dad was coming to take away the skid steer. I just knew that Samuel would not call ahead but would just pull in there and take it.

Mark was devastated. I could hardly stand it.

"Mom, I really thought that Dad changed, but now this? I guess he is still the same old dad." My grown son sobbed into the phone.

I wept with him, my heart breaking with his.

———————

It was an immediate relief to have Samuel gone. In less than twenty-four hours, I felt free again. I didn't know what was going to happen, but I figured that I would have some time to come up with a plan. Samuel would be gone for at least a month, and that would give me time to go to counseling and seek advice from them and also do a lot of praying.

A few days went by, and I didn't hear anything from Mark or Samuel. I spent time praying for both of them. I cried out to God for Samuel to find repentance and a genuine change of heart. I prayed for Mark to be filled with God's grace and protection. During the night before Samuel left, I had snuck out to his truck and took the pistol under out of the back seat and hid it in the house.

I finally called Samuel to see if he was on his way to Florida yet. He sounded so happy, but it was a strange kind of happiness. It was just like old times, when he was able to make all of us feel bad, and then he would be in a strange euphoric high of his own.

"So I guess you are on your way to Florida?" I asked, carefully making small talk while trying to figure out where his head was at.

"Oh no! I got the skid steer, and I'm coming back home."

With crystal clarity, I felt the strength of God rising up in me. At that moment, I was strong and bold again, and I said to him with a steady voice, "Samuel, you are not coming home. You have abused the kids, and you just said you want to kill me. No. You are not coming home. If I so much as see your truck on the road in front of my house, I am going to call the police."

He laughed, which unnerved me. "Well then, I'm just going to go stay with your sister. They'll make up a bed for me until you get your act together."

I pulled myself together. "No. That is too close. And you better not just show up there. You need to call and ask them first before you just show up."

I hung up and quickly called Jo. I told her what I had said to Samuel and warned her that he was planning to stay with them. So her husband called Samuel and told him that it would be best if he did not come there. He told Samuel that I needed some time and that he needed to find some other place to go.

I was so grateful for their support; I don't know what I would have done if they had not sensed the urgency of our situation. If I had let Samuel come back, I don't believe I would be alive today.

Anna and I | One year after leaving Samuel

Scream

So that one day a hundred years from now

Another sister will not have to dry her tears

Wondering where in history she lost her voice.

—Jasmin Kaur

II.

THE FIGHT FOR FREEDOM

The next week I went and got a restraining order for the kids and me. The grace and strength of God was so real. Without any contact with Samuel, I could see more clearly. I could see how he had started controlling me early on in our dating years. I could see how I allowed his emotions to trap me, allowing his issues to become my own.

My sister helped me write Samuel a final letter. I told him that I was not making any more demands on him, but that I was going to continue to go to counseling, and I was also putting the kids in counseling. I wished him all the best, but I was done with trying to work things out.

I was still beaten down emotionally, and I had low self-esteem, but through counseling and the many people in my life who encouraged me, I started taking tiny steps forward. Determined to follow through and become victorious one day at a time, I refused to become a victim of what I had suffered all those years. Pastor Nate hired me to help with janitorial work at the church. It wasn't much, but it gave me confidence that God would provide for us.

That year, all of my kids were able to come home for Christmas. There is no greater joy for a mom than when all of her kids are under her roof. I slept extra peaceful those nights. I had grown up celebrating Christmas, and while we were dating, Samuel always gave me Christmas presents. Even though his family did not celebrate, Samuel promised me that we would celebrate it, but like all the other promises he made me, he didn't keep his word.

When we got married, Samuel decided that we could not celebrate Christmas anymore and our children never knew what a Christmas could be like. So this was the first time we all celebrated Christmas together as a family. Having my kids all around me, seeing them all laughing and having a good time, made it the best Christmas I could possibly imagine.

David had signed up to join the Army, and during the holidays, Mark told me that he was planning to join the Army, too. He planned to go sign up right after the Christmas holidays. He was on his way to the army recruitment center when a Marine recruiter stopped him, and he then decided to join the Marines. I would have two sons in our nation's armed forces, fighting to defend our country's freedom.

The thought of my sons being in harm's way brought a cold chill to my heart, but I was also so incredibly proud of both of them. I soaked in my time with each of my children that Christmas, sensing that life was going to change once again, for all of us.

———————

I needed to get a job. The settlement money from the accident was running out, and Samuel didn't pay any financial support. To give me time to find a job, I went into the DHS (Department of Human Services) and filled out paperwork for a cash and food stamps program. Then I had to go to Michigan Works. The ladies there helped me write up a resume, even though I didn't have any work history. This was just all so new to me. I enrolled in workshops, and I applied for jobs every week.

One day when I came to a workshop, my sponsor told me that some recruiters from a company were here hiring. She suggested I go over and talk to them. I was so happy to hear that! Would this be a full-time job? I went in and introduced myself. They handed me some tests to take. I sat down full of eagerness and anxiousness. I thought the tests seemed pretty easy. Apparently, I passed them with flying colors! They told me I was hired as an inspector at an automobile factory in my town.

And just like that, I was a woman with a real job, just minutes from our home. The hiring people suggested that I buy a pair of steel-toed boots and safety glasses. Feeling elated, I told my sponsor. She gave me her number, said to call her if I ever needed more help, and expressed how proud she was of me. Full of confidence, I headed to the store and bought the shoes and glasses. I was so excited to go home. I couldn't wait for the kids to come home from school so I could tell them.

They were so excited. I told them I might even

get called in that night. And sure enough, later that evening, I got a phone call. They needed more help at inspections.

I was so nervous as I headed to the plant. Before I could go into the plant, I had to watch several videos. They were all about plant rules and safety procedures. Inspections was easy work, and I really enjoyed it. I felt proud to be supporting the kids all by myself.

It was so strange to be working in a plant environment. I wasn't used to being around men that much. I had always been shy and quiet around men. Even though I now wore jeans and T-shirts, I still saw myself as an Amish woman. When you have been raised Amish and always dress differently than the *Englisha*, it is just engrained so deeply inside of you. So even though I had been dressing differently for a few years already, I still defined myself by the culture I came from.

As an Amish woman, I was raised to lower my eyes when speaking with any man. At first, their raunchy comments and general enthusiasm made me blush, so they teased me. It was a hard habit to break, but with time, I got over some of my shyness, and my job became much easier as I learned to talk face to face and make eye contact when speaking to the men that I worked with. They even cleaned up their language around me and began to respect me. Eventually, I made friends and learned how to interact with men in a healthier way.

———————

I finally decided to file for divorce. Samuel was not doing anything positive to show that he wanted to reconcile. He started going to different Amish communities to trash me and my family's name and to try to get pity for his situation. At this point, I really didn't care, since those who meant the most to me knew the truth.

With all the abuse my children and I had suffered, divorce was the best solution. Mark told Anna later that after he went through his medical exams to join the Marine Corps, he was asked to provide them with his missing medical records. "What records?" he said. "I don't have anything." They replied, "Well, you should have additional records because of all the healed fractures throughout your body." That's when

Mark knew that his many beatings had broken several bones that had healed all on their own, without ever receiving any medical attention.

While I felt horrible for everything my children had been exposed to when I hadn't been strong enough, from here on out, I was looking forward. I was taking action. I was now strong enough. I had heard about an attorney from another lady in our church, so I got her number to call her office and made an appointment. From the moment I met her, I felt safe committing this part of my life in her hands. She wanted to hear my story.

I wasn't talking long before she said, "Anna, you need to write a book!"

"Oh, I don't know," I said, looking bashfully down at the floor.

"There are other women out there in abusive situations, and they need to hear your story so they know they have a way out."

I couldn't imagine it then, but eight years later, I would finally find the strength to write my story.

Filing for divorce was another step in cutting the ties to our horrible past and paving the way for a future full of freedom. My attorney was everything and more that I could've asked for. She acted as my guardian angel, comforting me and giving good advice. She was always just a phone call away to answer all my questions and fears.

It should have been a quick divorce, but, of course, Samuel did not cooperate. We had to reschedule court hearings many times because he didn't let his attorney know that he was not coming.

At our first meeting with the Friend of the Court, Samuel showed up with two of his brothers-in-law. He thought he could bring them into the meeting as his council and intimidate me into giving up on getting a divorce. When I walked into the courthouse, I saw Samuel, for the first time in nine months, and the two men that accompanied him standing off to one side. I went through security, then quickly got in an elevator and went up a few floors just to get some space.

I was shaking so hard. I called my attorney right away, since she still wasn't there. She calmed me down. She told me to stay in one of the waiting rooms till she got there. Once she arrived, I felt so much safer with her by my side.

The Friend of the Court told Samuel that his relatives were not allowed in the meeting, only his attorney. So he said that he was going to represent himself. The first thing on the discussion was how much Samuel was going to start paying per month. He wouldn't give a straight answer. Instead he pulled out a credit card statement and laid it on the table. In an accusing tone, he announced that I had opened a credit account in his name, and he was clearly ready for the court to criminalize me for it.

I had been using the credit card to buy groceries and clothes for the kids. Samuel thought he was going to get me in trouble for doing this, but instead, they told him that because we were still married, it was not considered fraud. Besides, they told him that because he wasn't paying me any child support, I had to have some way to take care of the children. That was the moment when Samuel changed his tune. Now he wanted an attorney. He thought he could control this, but once he realized he couldn't and they were holding him accountable, he got angry.

I could see his anger, but I felt safe with all

of the others in the room. My attorney advised me to stay in the courthouse for a while, just to make sure Samuel would be gone once I went to leave. She then followed me to my car. She told me that nothing scared her more than someone like Samuel who was obviously unstable and what she called a "bible thumper."

"Anna, you can't be too careful. When these bible thumpers use the Bible to condemn other people, they're always the most dangerous ones. You can't trust Samuel." She had a friend who had a bomb planted on their car by a "bible thumper," so she checked our cars before we left.

To see if we could reconcile or at least come to an agreement for child support, my attorney set up an appointment for Samuel and me to meet with the Friend of the Court. Surprisingly, Samuel showed up. While I was still nervous to be around him, the presence of an authority figure calmed me down.

Samuel opened up the dialogue by accusing me of not submitting to his authority, like that was going to criminalize me in a court of law. When asked what he would commit to paying to help with the kids, he would not agree to any amount. The Friend of the Court explained to Samuel that the kids were his responsibility. He told him it was not fair to expect me to support them alone, especially considering I had always been a homemaker and had no way of furthering my education in order to get a good job, but it didn't matter what the Friend of the Court said, Samuel still wouldn't commit to paying child support. He was openly rude and aggressive throughout the mediation process, and it did not take the Friend of the Court long to see how abusive he was.

Once Samuel hired an attorney, he and his attorney decided that they wanted our children to testify in our case. I didn't want to ask our children to do this and my attorney agreed, but they wouldn't back down. We finally agreed that the older ones could testify if they wanted to, but not the younger kids. Mark and David were both in the military, so they couldn't come. Anna, Sammy, and Mose said they would testify.

I dreaded the upcoming court hearing so much that it made me sick. I hated that the children had to revisit the memories of how they were abused, then talk about it in court in front of other people. I didn't want to put them through that. We were reliving all of the trauma, and it wasn't fair to the children.

I was so relieved when my attorney told me that Sammy and Mose would only testify in front of the judge in his chambers. I really liked our judge. He was so nice and caring. He talked so calmly to Sammy and Mose when we met with him. He told them that they didn't have to see their dad. Everyone in the court would be able to see them testify on a monitor, but they wouldn't be able to see into the courtroom.

The day of the hearing finally arrived. It was a breezy, sunny day that contrasted starkly with the weight of what I was facing. I drove to the courthouse with the children, my thoughts in a whirlwind. There was a possibility that Samuel wouldn't show up, and everything would be delayed yet again.

Sammy talked with the judge first. He told him how he feared his dad's beatings and the size of some of the boards that his dad had used to beat him with. He shared the story of when Samuel made Mark hold him down while his dad beat him. I sat in the courtroom, watching my young son on the monitor as tears streamed down my face.

Mose testified next. One of his first memories, when he was like four or five years old, was when he was playing outside and his ball rolled over behind the shop. He went running over to get it and heard terrible screaming coming from inside the shop. He slowly made his way around and peeked in the door. He saw his dad with an air nail gun screaming at Mark and chasing after him, shooting nails at him.

Everyone in the courtroom was horrified. Even though this had happened without my knowing, I had a clear picture of Mose as that little boy who was standing just outside of the shop, shaking in fear at the sight. Samuel had occasionally killed animals with a nail gun, but I never knew he shot at his own son. I felt faint as I wept.

I glanced out of the corner of my eye at Samuel. He sat there shaking his head with a smug smile on his face, looking so self-righteous. That blew my mind. What reality was he living in? How could he not see the pain that his actions caused?

Even Samuel's attorney looked horrified and said, "This is just terrible."

My attorney just looked at him and said, "You haven't even heard the worst parts yet. Wait till you hear what his daughter Anna has to say."

Next was Anna. If she was shaking or nervous,

I couldn't tell. She seemed as bold and fearless as the day that she stopped Sammy's beating. She swore to tell the truth and nothing but.

Anna shared several aspects of how abusive Samuel was. She explained to the judge that because I was raised as an Amish wife, I was told not to question or go against what my husband said or did. It was not allowed. She told him how he would scold me after getting necessary groceries, always accusing me of spending too much. Then when we ate, he filled his plate first and made sure he got what he wanted before the rest of us were allowed to eat.

Anna told the judge about the beatings of the little ones when they were about two years old in order to "break their wills." These beatings could last for several hours, intermittently, until the toddler would be completely compliant.

I could hear a trembling sound in Anna's voice as she continued. She said that because Jake had been a very fussy baby, Samuel would hold him tight and put his large hand over Jake's mouth till he started turning blue to get him to stop crying. It was so hard to listen to Anna's testimony. I wanted to run out of the courthouse, screaming. There were tears in Anna's eyes now, but she wanted to keep going. That was my daughter; she refused to back down even though it was taking everything she had to talk about the abuse that she and her siblings had experienced on a daily basis. It was all they had known.

None of the children had heard each other's testimonies, but similar things had made a clear impression on each of them. Anna described the big, thick paddles that Samuel used to beat the children with. She talked about the various scenarios of the beatings that she witnessed. When the judge asked her about the abuse she experienced, she described an instance when her dad had knocked her out by hitting her across the face when she was fifteen years old.

Once the judge heard Anna's testimony, he looked over at me with compassion and said, "I don't even need to hear what you have to say. I have heard enough."

The validation I felt from hearing those words come out of the judge's mouth was so overwhelming. I just sat there and cried. After all those years of being told I was wrong and crazy and evil and no good and spending too much money and I didn't measure up to other women and I didn't know what I was talking about, the truth finally came out. The realization that the judge saw and believed the truth meant more than I could even begin to explain in words.

Many times I had thought I might be crazy. After all, Samuel told me that I imagined things and remembered things the wrong way. Now I wondered how I didn't see all the things that Samuel was doing and hiding from me. I wondered how no one else saw that something wrong was happening in our family, why no one said anything.

How could I not see how traumatized the children felt and acted? How could I not see all of the abuse? I guess I still don't really know everything. Other than while you are the one being abused, it is hard to see what is going on. It is hard to separate yourself, to think or see clearly. You have to get away from it to see it for what it really is.

The judge required both Samuel and I to get a psychological evaluation. I wasn't afraid to go get one, so I made an appointment with one of the recommended psychologists right away. It was a totally different visit than I had ever had before. I had gone to see a counselor, but this was completely different.

I enjoyed the visit. It lasted about an hour. He asked me a lot of different questions, not particularly about any one thing. Then I was free to go.

Later, the psychologist called my attorney to tell her how it went, and she also got a copy of the evaluation. He told my attorney that I am an amazing woman.

When I heard about their conversation and read my evaluation, I couldn't believe what I was hearing and seeing. Deep down inside, I was still afraid that I was crazy or that someone wouldn't believe me. It felt so good to be validated once again.

———————

Yet, my battle still wasn't over.

It seemed like it was never going to be over. Going to court on the appointed dates continued for over a year. Most of the time, Samuel did not show up. He didn't even contact his attorney and let him know he wasn't showing up. Instead, he just harassed my attorney, writing long letters full of threats and biblical condemnation, so she took on her own personal protective measures during the year that the trial drug on. It was all very taxing on my mental state. I just wanted this chapter of my life to be closed.

I was shocked when I received support from Samuel's own family. One of Samuel's sisters wrote me a letter. While she didn't approve of my filing for divorce, she did understand my frustration with her brother. She told me that all his life Samuel never faced up to any of his problems. He would always try to run from them and blame others. She confirmed much of the troubling behavior that I knew about my soon-to-be ex-husband.

I prepared myself to be rejected by some members of his family and mine, because some of my relatives believed that I should never get a divorce. I had already gone through a rejection when Samuel decided we were leaving the Amish, and I still carried those wounds deep in my soul. But at this point, being rejected by family was not going to stop me from fighting for my freedom.

Even without all of the physical and sexual abuse, I knew that I had grounds for divorce based on the emotional and verbal abuse alone. With renewed courage, I kept moving forward.

Finally, my final court date with Samuel arrived. I put on a soft, blue floral dress that morning and debated over whether I should wear a string of pearls around my neck. I decided against it. I still wasn't sure what jewelry to accessorize with.

I met my attorney at her office before driving to the courthouse because she needed to prepare me for the day. She wore a dark-colored pantsuit, with a pair of heels. She always wore heels.

Each time we were finished with another court hearing with Samuel, she got down on the ground, in her heels, to check under our vehicles for any bombs that could be planted there, and then she got back up, dusted off her knees, and carried on like everything was fine. She was the definition of a classy, strong woman, and her example taught me how to be the same.

To my relief, Samuel showed up for the final hearing. Each time I saw him, I felt sick to my stomach and it was hard to steady myself, but today, I prayed this awful nightmare was all going to be over.

After what felt like hours, the trial began. The judge reviewed everything in front of him that pertained to the outstanding issues and began with the custody agreement. He didn't hesitate as he gave me full custody of the children. A huge wave of relief washed over me. No one expected the judge to rule in Samuel's favor, but it was such a relief to hear a final decision that would protect the children from living under the constant threat of Samuel's abuse ever again. Then he moved on to the child support decision.

Samuel refused to document any type of income at all, since that is normally what the court uses to determine the amount of child support that is owed. The court acknowledged that I had an unfair advantage, having being a stay-at-home mom for all those years with no chance to get a degree or learn skills for jobs. The judge ordered that Samuel pay $500 a month for all five children and another $500 for spousal support.

While that was hardly enough child support to provide for all of the children, it would help. Little did I know that I would never see the support that Samuel had been ordered to give me—instead, he would later be arrested and spend time in jail for his refusal to pay. After a family member bailed him out, he disappeared off the grid, and I continued to work to provide everything the children needed.

Then I heard the words that set me free at last, before the judge hammered the gavel. In the case of Anna Schwartz vs. Samuel Troyer, a divorce was granted.

I was no longer married to Samuel Troyer. I was a divorced woman. Such a huge weight lifted from me. It had felt like I was bound by heavy chains, and suddenly, they just broke apart and fell off me. I was free to lift my hands, to spin around, to dance, laugh, and LIVE.

As I was driving home, I turned on the radio and the song "This Is the Day" by Lincoln Brewster came on. I had to pull over as I wept tears of joy. I knew that God planned for me to hear that song at that moment.

I'm casting my cares aside
I'm leaving my past behind
I'm putting my fears aside
I'm leaving my doubts behind
I'm giving my hopes and dreams to You, Jesus
I'm reaching my hands to Yours
Believing there's so much more
Knowing that all You have in store for me is good

"This Is the Day"
Song Lyrics by Paul Baloche
Performed by Artist Lincoln Brewster

12.

HELLO PEACE

I slowed down the car as I drove around the last tree-lined curve before I got to my oldest sister's house. Mom has been living in the guest portion of Irvin and Esther's house; she moved in when Dad died so Esther could take care of her. It'd been so long since I'd seen Mom, and now I was going there to celebrate her eightieth birthday.

The car pulled into the gravel driveway, making a crunching sound with the tiny stones underneath my tires, and I looked around at the buggies parked by the barn. No one else drove here in a car but me. I pulled around so as to not park too close to the house or the buggies, out of respect for my Amish family. I was still excommunicated and they had to still practice the *Shunning* if they wanted to remain in good standing with the church. Going to their house to visit them was allowed, as long as I did not park my car by the house or eat with them at the same table.

I checked my reflection in the mirror and applied some chapstick to my lips. I'd kept my appearance plain today, no makeup, and I picked a solid-colored dress with a long skirt to wear. My bangs fell across my forehead, and I wondered what Mom would think of my short haircut.

The memory of Saturday afternoons as a child at home came rushing back to me. After heating the water on the stove, Mom would help us girls wash our hair in the sink. Then she would comb my long brown hair, brush it, divide it into sections, and braid it. Even though it hurt a little when she combed out the tangles, I loved the feeling of having my hair braided. My sister Josephine never liked having her hair braided, though. She would cry and tell Mom, "You're purposely pulling my hair; it hurts so bad!" I looked up to see her standing by the door now, waiting for me, a warm smile on her face.

Two of my sisters greeted me at the door, and I

noticed a couple of my great-nieces scampering away after I caught them peeking shyly around the corner at their *Englisha* Great Aunt Anna.

"Is my Anna here?" Mom called from the living room.

"It's me, Mom," I answered back, taking off my shoes and placing them on the rug by the entryway. Esther always kept a clean house, no dirty shoes were allowed in the living room. She had been married to an Amish bishop, Irvin, for over thirty years, and they now had married sons and daughters of their own, with grandchildren.

The aroma of Esther's cooking made my mouth water. I could still hear the scampering sounds of the children as they peeked at me from the other room. I caught a glimpse of little Erma, Rosie's daughter, and smiled. "How old are you?" I asked her in Pennsylvania Dutch, and she held up seven fingers, her face brightening with a smile when she realized that I spoke her language.

Mom sat in a small, dark blue recliner in the corner of the living room. She looked up when she saw me walk into the living room. She said nothing to me but tilted her head to the side with a gentle smile and reached for me. I went to her, like a little girl with her freshly done braids, and knelt beside her chair.

"Mom." I felt my eyes getting moist as I took in her withered, eighty-year-old body, before I leaned into her open arms that pulled me into a tight hug. Her strength held me there, with a love that enveloped my soul.

Her papery soft cheek was against my hair when she whispered in my ear, "I finally have my Ann back."

I held back the sobs that threatened to burst from my chest and closed my eyes. This is what it feels like to come home: like the comfort of an extra pair of warm socks under the covers on a cold winter's night, like the gift of the first ray of sun that touches my face in the morning, and like being in the body of a young child who is picked up and kissed after falling down. For just a moment, it was as though time had never passed and the nightmares had never happened because I was in Mom's arms, safe and completely loved. Peace flooded my soul.

Esther served chicken soup with homemade noodles for lunch. I ate separately from everyone else because of the *Shunning*, savoring each bite of the soup, not minding that I sat alone. There's nothing like homemade chicken noodle soup. Mom taught all of us girls to make homemade noodles. It always started with preparing the house for noodle-making day. First, we would go upstairs to sweep our attic and mop it until every inch of the space was completely clean. After the floor was dry, we laid clean, white sheets across the wooden floorboards.

The noodle-making experience was satisfying. I helped Mom pull and knead the elastic dough before placing it under a towel in a warm area for half an hour. She'd fasten the heavy, stainless steel noodle maker on the edge of the table before dividing the dough into softball-sized lumps and flattening them with a wooden rolling pin into long, thin strips. Carefully, we draped the strips of dough over a wooden dryer rack until they were semi-dry. Mom would feed the semi-dry strips of dough into the noodle maker while slowly turning the handle, and we would stand in line on the other side, holding up the corners of our clean white aprons and letting the noodles fall in until we had a nice apron full. With our apron skirts full of freshly cut noodles, we gingerly walked up the steps to the attic and gently spread them out on the white bedsheets. After the noodles dried overnight, we bagged them and tied each bag shut with a white twist tie. Some of the noodles were for our family, but Mom sold most of them to her egg customers.

I helped my sisters wash the dishes after the meal was over before gathering around Mom in the living room to sing songs. We sang from memory, yodeling in harmony to the chorus.

Over a bowl of popcorn, Mom began telling us a story. "When I was a teenager in the *Rumspringa*, I was going to walk home from the singing on a Sunday evening. But there was a guy." She held up her finger to let us all know that this part of the story was important. "Well, I don't remember what his name was, but he offered me a ride. I tried to refuse because it was a few miles out of the way for him, and I thought, 'now why would he want to take me home,' but anyway, he insisted, so I got in his buggy."

I glanced around the room at my sisters, curious to know if any of them knew the ending of this story, but by the anticipation on their faces, I guessed that they didn't, and we all leaned in together to hear what happened next.

"Well, it was a good thing I got into that guy's

buggy." Mom chuckled. "About halfway home, there was a huge bull that had gotten loose from our neighbor's fence and, boy, was he angry. He ran after the buggy and tried to attack the horse, but that horse ran faster than the bull and got us out of there in a hurry! You know, I thought if I had walked home that night, that bull would have killed me! I was shaken up for the rest of the night." She shook her head. There was a murmur across the room as we all sighed a breath of relief in unison.

Mom always had a knack for telling us stories that had us sitting on the edge of our seats until she got to the ending. On sewing days, we used to gather around her and the treadle sewing machine, kneeling on the floor, and while she sewed, she would tell us stories. She told us stories that she remembered by heart from *Old Mother West Wind* books or she'd make up a story from her own imagination.

She would also let us take turns poking the edge of a stiff piece of paper by the sewing machine wheel, as it made a satisfying noise when it hit the spokes. It was fascinating to watch Mom as her feet pumped the pedal up and down, the wheel going fast, the spokes a blur, and the fabric slipping rapidly through the sewing machine.

The night slowly stole the light from the room. Irvin lit two kerosene lamps, and Esther offered to make more popcorn for everyone, but we shook our heads because it was time to bring our time together to a close. I lingered behind as everyone took turns telling Mom goodbye. I didn't want the day to be over.

"My Ann, thank you for coming." She pulled me in for a hug again, and then she held my hand. I waited, because I knew she had something to say.

"I don't believe in divorce." She paused. "But in your situation, you had no choice but to save the kids and yourself from harm." She paused again and looked into my eyes with a fierce love that lit up her own.

I choked. "Thank you, Mom. You don't know . . . that just means so much to me."

She squeezed my hand. "You have my full support, Anna."

Peace washed over me at the sound of my mom's words. Peace was worth every struggle I encountered to face fear. Peace was worth everything it took to find my freedom. As I looked into Mom's eyes, I knew that I didn't have to be afraid anymore.

The first thing that really stood out to me, once Samuel was no longer in our lives, was the peace. I had a new, constant calm in my life. When I had been living with Samuel, I'd always been waiting for a bad storm to break out, because one was always brewing.

It could be calm for a day, sometimes several days or even a week, but I always knew the storm clouds were there, just over the horizon. I knew it was coming; I just never knew if it would be a thunderstorm or a tornado. I had never realized how stressful it was to live like that. Now, to have that gone forever, words can't begin to describe how different our lives were.

One day I checked my mailbox and saw an envelope with familiar handwriting on it. Nervously, because I still never knew who might write to me to condemn my choices, I took the mail inside. I opened the letter and sat down in my recliner. It was from my sister-in-law.

Dear Anna,

I hope yous and the children are doing good these days. I'm writing to you because Samuel wanted me to share some things with you and he didn't want to tell you himself. He's been telling me about some of his earliest memories and some other things. When he was 4 years old, he saw Dad and Mom fighting. Mom got a kitchen knife out and chased Dad with it and then he picked her up and threw her across the room. Sam remembers that Mom got up and came to him and cried. You know how Dad and Mom were with each other, they fought a lot. Since Samuel was the youngest, he was around it the most after the rest of us got married and it troubled him a great deal. I think that's why he had some mental problems. The other thing that Samuel told me was that he practiced *bestiality for years while he was living on the farm at home. He said that he did it with every animal they had. He confessed it to me and he told me that he wanted me to tell you and he wants to ask for your forgiveness.*

I finished reading the letter and slowly folded it. I wanted to throw up. The letter made me feel sick through my whole body and soul. I didn't know why Samuel wanted his sister to tell me all of these things.

Perhaps it was a cry for sympathy with the hope that I would take him back. Maybe it was an excuse for the way he behaved. Whatever the reason, I couldn't let it take away the peace that I had found.

I felt some compassion for Samuel as I put the letter back in the envelope. It was clearer to me now than before that he was still a hurting boy on the inside of a grown man. The wounds from his childhood turned him into the raging abuser that I lived with. The phrase was true—*hurt people hurt people.*

But I could not be Samuel's therapist or his doctor or his savior, and now I was no longer his wife.

This was no longer my fight. I let it go. And I moved on.

————————

I went to see Mom again on my birthday, and she told me the story of my birth. I was born at the end of the summer when the last of the harvest from the garden still needed to be put away for winter.

"That morning I was in labor, but I told Dad to go to work anyway," she recalled. "I had two bushels of tomatoes waiting to be made into juice. Your older sisters, Esther and Rachel, washed all of them while I cut them into quarters and filled the big stock pots. We had a kerosene stove out in the wash house where I carried them between contractions."

I could picture Mom now, with a large pregnant middle, waddling out to the wash house with large kettles full of chopped tomatoes. "Had you been having some false labor with me before then?" I interjected.

"Sort of, but I just knew how long labor usually takes so I wanted to get this done before you were born." Mom laughed, and then she continued on with the story.

"After boiling the tomatoes, I let them cool while the girls helped me set up the hand crank juicer. Do you remember it?"

"Yep." I smiled. I used the same juicer to make tomato sauce from tomatoes after I grew up and had my own garden. Everything Mom taught me to do, I'd done with my own children. She just wasn't around to see that because of the *Shunning*.

"Well, after that, I poured the tomato juice into quart jars and boiled them in a water bath to seal the lids," she explained, as though she was reliving each moment of that day. "It felt so good to get all of that done. My contractions were much harder now and getting very regular, so I sent Esther over to the neighbors to call an *Englisha* driver to take me to the hospital. She also called Dad at work and let him know that I was in labor."

I was starting to wonder if Mom ever made it to the hospital to give birth, because it always took a while before a driver would show up.

"Once the driver came, I had to take all of the other children to Uncle Joe's house before heading to Parkview hospital in Fort Wayne, Indiana." She paused when she saw the look on my face and chuck-led. "Oh, I made it. It wasn't long after I got there till you were born, though. I got there just in the nick of time."

I shook my head, amazed by my mom. She got all of her tomato juice canning done and gave birth to a baby, all in a days' time. What a woman.

"And you know, when I came home from the hospital with you, your brother Leroy would not even come look at you. No sirree!" She shook her head and chuckled again. "He said there was no way this baby could be a girl. He said that this baby had to be a boy because he already had four sisters, and he was out-numbered. Oh my, he was so mad that you weren't a boy! Now he had five sisters!"

I thought of my own daughter Anna when she wanted a sister, and I kept having baby boys. I mar-veled over the ways that our lives were full of so many parallels.

Mom adjusted her weight in the chair before she continued. She always made me think that she was going to leave me on a cliffhanger, not knowing how the story ended. "A few days later when I went to the bedroom to check on you, there was Leroy. He was standing by the crib, holding you."

I thought about the ways that Leroy still cared for me and looked out for me, especially since my divorce. He wept when he found out what I had been through, and he told me how sorry he was for everything that had happened to me. My brother never got a brother because Mom had one more daughter after me before she quit having babies. Maybe he was such a good husband because of all the sisters he had, and eventually, he had two sons of his own.

"Your great-grandma was from the Amish in Canada. She was a big-boned woman and loved horses. Her husband passed away at a young age from a farming accident, and she was left to raise their six children alone. She trained horses for income and always drove a really nice horse!"

"Wow," I murmured. The women who came before me were strong and innovative. Nothing could stop them. Then I asked her, "Weren't my great-great grandparents from France?"

"Yes." Mom nodded. "Here, hand me that box on the *shankly* (a piece of furniture)."

I found the one she was pointing to and gave it to her. She opened it and pulled out a small black-

and-white Polaroid.

"See, that's their farm in Alsace. This is where they made cheese." She pointed to the small wash-house near the barn. "Chris Delagrange, that's the name of your great-great grandfather."

Mom's last name was Delagrange when she married my dad, Chris Schwartz. When I was a girl, I learned how to speak and yodel in Swiss from my dad, who was born in Berne, Indiana.

Swiss, Canadian, and French blood all ran together in my ancestry and that fascinated me. I gathered all of the information that Mom was sharing with me and tucked it away in my mind so I could share it with my children.

These stories were part of their lives, too, and I wanted them to live on so they could share them with their children one day. That was how the legacy of our family would continue on. This was the legacy that they could be proud of.

———

Three years later, Mom had a stroke that left her partially paralyzed and with a broken hip. After another stroke left her with a speech impediment, I moved close by so I could help take care of her.

During the last eight months of her life, I spent several nights each week with Mom. Some days I drove over and took her out for lunch. She stopped recognizing me as she lost her memory, and for several months she didn't seem to know who I was anymore, but she would tell Esther that she really likes "that woman."

About a month before she died, she recognized me again when I came one evening to take care of her. "Oh . . . my Ann . . . my Ann is here!" She stammered excitedly.

She wanted to go sit out on the front porch, so I took her out there. It was such a nice evening. The setting sun cast its long, warm rays across us as we sat with each other, and Mom talked more than I'd heard her talk in months, despite her speech impediment. She asked about my children, and I told her everything that was happening in their lives. She was proud to hear they were doing well for themselves.

After a while, she said, "Let's go in and ask Esther if we can go out for breakfast. I want to take you out for breakfast in the morning!"

I blinked back tears as I rolled Mom's wheelchair into the house to find Esther.

I remembered the day that Samuel called me to tell me that we were leaving the Amish, and I feared that I'd be pulled away from my family forever, but here I was now, with my mom.

I had peace in my heart, and I knew it would be with me during whatever lay ahead. It's a peace that no one will ever be able to take away from me.

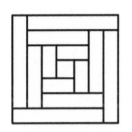

AFTERWORD

I'm Anna's oldest daughter. In the book, you got to know me as her namesake. In real life, I've changed my name to Meg, which isn't an Amish name. I used to be embarrassed by how I grew up, but I'm not anymore. Now I'm proud of my heritage. I would not be the woman I am today without it, nor would I be who I am without the influence of my parents, and for that, I am eternally grateful.

Four years ago, I was sitting on a giant rock beside the Nile River in Uganda, Africa. I'd flown there to paint a large mural in a primary boarding school. *Yes, sometimes plain little girls grow up and be-*

come colorful artists.

As I sat on the rock, watching the rising fog reveal Ugandan fisherman in their little wooden boats out on the river, I had an epiphany. I'd just spent a sleepless night tossing and turning in a small hut on top of the hill beside the river. I'd asked God what my life was for and why I was really here. Struggling with the pain of my childhood and my own divorce and wrestling with questions that I couldn't answer, I felt a deep, aching loneliness that wouldn't subside, no matter how busy I kept myself or how many places I traveled across the world.

Maybe it should be a shocker that after ten years of therapy, I still questioned my purpose. I still struggled with the pain of abuse in my upbringing. I felt conflicted about my divorce and the weight of responsibility for raising my daughter on my own. As I sat there, I questioned God. *Why, God, does there have to be so much suffering in this world? Why?* I had so many unanswered questions.

Perhaps, it was the way the water churned and thundered over the rocks just beyond the fishermen in the river that morning. The white water rapids were a site of terrifying yet wondrous beauty. Beautiful to look at, yet deathly to get caught in. In a place where danger and peace intertwined, I found myself entering a door beyond my questions.

I opened my Bible on the rock in front of me. The phrase I read that morning was a simple one that I had read a thousand times before, but this time I received a fresh revelation.

"All things work together for good." ROMANS 8:28

In the wind that cannot be seen by the eye and only known by the spirit, I heard a quiet whisper that settled the noise inside of my mind: "***All things*** work together for ***good***. Don't try to figure it out. Goodness is at work here. Trust."

I closed my eyes. "Everything that I don't understand is going to somehow work together for good. Focus on the *good,* now. *Good* things are coming. And *good* things are already here. Look around and see the *good.*"

Letting my questions hang in the air, I left the rock to finish painting the mural. I didn't completely understand the message I had received, but I felt hope. I saw so much good around me, despite the depravity and pain that was also present. I saw goodness in the children's wide smiles as they danced their own traditional Ugandan dance. I tasted goodness in the steaming bowls of rice with specially prepared fish, probably caught by the fishermen that I watched on the river earlier that morning.

Seeing the good wasn't about sugarcoating anything. It was about recognizing both the good and the bad and choosing to focus on the good. What we focus on, expands. What we focus on, we become. Nothing is required from us to see and experience this goodness—it's been here all along.

When my mom finished writing the initial draft of her book, she shared it with me. At the time, I was traveling abroad once again for the summer, this time while having a tumultuous fling with a man twenty years my senior. Finally, I'd met someone who had completely swept me off of my feet. But something wasn't right about it. Something felt very wrong.

Initially, I felt flattered by his lavish attention, accompanied by generous gifts. It was an age-old sign of love bombing by a classic narcissist that I was blinded to. It didn't take very long for him to reveal who he really was, though. Not a month into our relationship, I wished I had never said yes to our first date. I wanted out. I wanted the relationship to be over. One minute I believed that he loved me, while the next moment, I was terrified of him. I felt helpless in a tangled web of poor choices. I knew that I had made the choices to get where I had gotten, and I felt trapped and lost.

As I read the entire length of my mom's personal story for the first time, my tears began falling. Like the brisk November air that constricts my chest when I jump out of a plane at 18,000 feet above sea level to go skydiving, the truth grabbed and opened my heart in a way that I could no longer be oblivious to. From my previous marriage to my current fling, I was repeating the same dysfunctional relationship patterns that my mom had been trapped in. They were patterns that were rooted in fear.

I was her. And she was me.

Through witnessing the turmoil and victory of my mom's journey, I was awakened to the truth of who I really was. Who she really was. We shared far more than our given birth name, Anna. We were both more than the choices we'd made and the hurt we'd experienced. Being plain and experiencing pain did not define who we were. And pain would not be the end of our story.

Through what felt like an eagle's-eye view, I could see the thread of love and light that was present in my mom's story and in my own, like an umbilical cord that extended from another realm. Even though our stories held pain, they also held hope, and it took the pain we experienced to find the strength to break generational chains and birth new life in our lives.

The true meaning of Jeremiah 1:5 awakened my heart: "Before I formed you in your mother's womb I knew you."

Before we came into this world, before we ever faced fear, we were known by pure love.

God is love. And human beings are made in the image of God; moreover, each of us are known by God before being placed in our mother's wombs. Our lives essentially began as a brilliant thought in the mind of a loving God. Therefore, we did not come into the world lacking anything. We were born from the fullness of divine love, with that love at the core of our being. We did not come from fear; we came into this world from love. Love is our truest identity.

We are more loved than we could ever comprehend. Jesus Christ revealed to us that the barrier of sin has been mended, realigning us with the truth of who we are. We're not irretrievably broken or without hope in a world full of suffering, condemned to miss the mark. Instead, we're a sign of something magnificent going on in the earth. When we align with the truth of who we really are, we go from glory to glory, discovering the height and depth of this divine mystery.

As though someone had struck a set of church bells in my soul, I suddenly had the clarity to know what I needed to do. The understanding of who I really am gave me strength to rise up, no longer held back by fear. I was ready to own my journey and my voice and my choices, all of it. My mom's strength and determination transferred to me, as though she was connected to me through an IV. I ended the toxic relationship that I was in and chose not to look back.

Together, my mom and I were being called to end a cycle of generational bondage to fear.

The fear that enticed us to settle for less.

The fear that caused us not to trust ourselves.

The fear that kept us silenced under a dirty

cloud of shame.

The fear that made us believe we were not worthy of love or belonging.

The fear that brainwashed us with the idea that God is against us, instead of FOR us.

Fear is a liar.

Perfect love, divine *teleios agape* love, is the antidote to fear. Like darkness melts when light shines into it, so fear dissolves in the presence of divine love.

It was 5 p.m. in East Germany where I was staying; 10 a.m. in Michigan. My mom was halfway through her morning shift. I picked up the phone and called her anyway.

"You have to publish your story, Mom. You have to. It's going to help so many women." My voice broke. "It will help someone who needs to hear your story. I know that, because your book just saved the first woman."

I paused. "Your book just saved me."

I told her how I found the strength I needed to end a dysfunctional relationship through reading her story. We cried together over the phone, as though half of the world was no longer between us.

After I got off of the phone, my tears and snot

continued to fall on the pebbled, patterned carpet of that small German room until they formed a puddle. Everything I'd worked so hard to build and everything I'd thought I wanted all seemed to crumble around me until it was nothing but dust.

Again, I heard the whisper. "Come. See. Now I will do a new thing. All things work together for good."

ACKNOWLEDGEMENTS

To Jesus Christ, my Lord and Savior. Once I had a breakthrough to see and feel your unconditional love and compassion for me, it filled me with a burning strength deep in my soul, and I have never doubted it was you who gave me the strength to not look back but to continue on into this life of freedom.

To my mom, who stood by me and loved me unconditionally. You gave me so much more than the gift of life, and I'll treasure it always as I pass your legacy of love and storytelling on to my children.

To my daughter Meg, who added over 20,000 words and many hours of her creativity to this book. You helped me tell my story—and our story. I'm so grateful that we got to work on this together. You are so much more than my daughter—you will always be my friend.

To each of my beloved children, who mean more than life to me. You are the reason I never gave up. I pray that I have shown you a better way. I'm not perfect, but I love each of you more than I'll ever be able to express.

To my sister Barbara, who was such a rock for me and gave me such good advice at a time when I couldn't see clearly. I'll never be able to thank you for everything you've done for me.

To my entire family, who have always loved me, no matter what. You are the best family a girl could ask for.

To my pastors, Nate and Wendy, who counseled me and helped me get through many tough times.

To my attorney, Kim, who was more than just an attorney, but a guardian angel and a true friend who created a safe space for me. You gave me courage to be strong. You also made me promise to write my story. It has taken a few years to be able to write it. Every time I started before, I would cry and cry, and I'd quit. But this time, it was different. I knew I was ready at last to tell my story. Here it is. I finally did it. I know you're proud of me.

GLOSSARY

A collection of Pennsylvania Dutch words and phrases that are used in this book, in order of appearance.

Gma — Sunday church

Schrift—The Bible

Prediger — Amish Preacher

Lots Hussa — A homemade pair of men's trousers.

Gott in Himmel — God in Heaven

"Wach auff." — "Wake up."

Dawdy Haus — Separate living quarters for elderly parents or other family members.

Ordnung — A set of rules an Amish Church lives by.

Englisha — Non-Anabaptist, English-speaking people.

Rumspringa — A period of time from 16–21 years of age when an Amish young person socializes and explores their options before choosing to become a member of the Amish church.

A Singing — When a group of young people get together to sing songs, a popular weekly activity during Amish Rumspringa in the 70s–90s. A few plain communities still host a weekly singing for their young people.

"Eyiyie!" — An expression that expresses amazement.

Following Church — The process of studying the eighteen Articles of Faith in order to become a member of the Amish church.

Shatz Banlah — A wide fabric belt.

Corner Table — The Bridal Table at a wedding.

"Vas is letz?" — "What's wrong?"

Phone shack — A small building that holds a phone, outside of an Amish home.

Excommunication — The action of officially excluding someone from participating in the Amish church or community.

Shunning — The rules that are followed once someone has been excommunicated: to persistently avoid, ignore, or reject the one that has left the Amish church.

Grosdawdy and Grosmommy — Grandpa and Grandma.

"Vas is des?" — "What is this?"

"Ich vill ein getrank." — "I want a drink."

"Bish to sure?" — "Are you sure?"

Shankly — A piece of living room furniture that looks similar to a buffet table.

MEET THE AUTHOR

Anna Schwartz, a mother of eight, a grand-mother to ten, and business owner from Michigan, found the strength to escape the clutches of domestic abuse. But before that, her tenacity followed her through over twenty moves across the United States.

Now more than ten years after escaping her twenty-four-year abusive marriage with nothing but a suitcase, Anna has found the courage to tell her story in the hopes of helping those like her who might be survivors or victims of abuse.

Part true-crime story and part Amish memoir, her story is an incredible journey that has left her readers spellbound. Anna hopes, more than anything, that the women reading her book will find their courage, trust their guts, and know that they no longer have to settle for being a victim.

While no longer a member of the Amish community, Anna spends her days chauffeuring the Amish locals to their essential needs and appointments. She loves to crochet, listen to audiobooks, cook the large traditional Amish meals she grew up with, and spend time with her true loves, her children and grandchildren.

CONNECT WITH ANNA

www.plainanna.com

MEET THE COAUTHOR

Born into a world without color, Meg broke out of the plain community as a renegade artist who colors the world. Meg Delagrange-Belfon is a free spirit who lives for the next adventure and enjoys spending time with her family. Meg is passionate about teaching others how to "live in color". She currently resides in Denver, Colorado with her husband and their blended family of five children. It has been a great honor for her to work on this book alongside her mother.

CONNECT WITH MEG

www.coloringspirit.com
www.blendedmix.life

Made in the USA
Columbia, SC
22 September 2021